HOW TO SUCCEED AT
RETAIL

HOW TO SUCCEED AT RETAIL

Winning case studies and strategies for retailers and brands

Keith Lincoln and Lars Thomassen

KOGAN PAGE

London and Philadelphia

First published in Great Britain and the United States in 2007 by Kogan Page Limited

120 Pentonville Road   525 South 4th Street, #241
London N1 9JN   Philadelphia PA 19147
United Kingdom   USA
www.kogan-page.co.uk

© Keith Lincoln, 2007

ISBN   978 0 7494 5016 8

British Library Cataloguing-in-Publication Data

A CIP record for this book is available from the British Library.

Library of Congress Cataloging-in-Publication Data

Lincoln, Keith.
   How to succeed at retail: winning case studies and strategies for retailers and brands/Keith Lincoln and Lars Thomassen.
      p. cm.
   Includes index.
   ISBN-13: 978-0-7494-5016-8
   ISBN-10: 0-7494-5016-9
1. Retail trade. 2. Brand name products. I. Title.
   HF5429.L5227 2007
   658.8'7--dc22
                                                   2007022195

Typeset by Saxon Graphics Ltd, Derby
Printed and bound in Great Britain by MPG Books Ltd, Bodmin, Cornwall

To our children: tomorrow's shoppers... and today's!

Contents

Preface... to succeed or not!

> To be or not to be... that is the question.
>
> *Hamlet* – William Shakespeare

Tibetan monks say their prayers by whirling wheels on which their prayers are inscribed, spinning the prayers into divine space. Sometimes a monk will keep a dozen or so prayer wheels rotating at the same time. Selling brands in today's retail environments must be a fairly similar experience!

Here we are again to talk to you about the world of brands and even more importantly the world of brands when they operate in retail environments and a world where they constantly try to succeed. Where they try 'to be or not to be'. This was the subject of our first book written with Anthony Aconis as co-author, *Retailization – Brand Survival in the Age of Retailer Power*, a book that has exceeded our expectations. A book that we're pleased to note has sold from Shanghai to California and is already entering its third print run, and has been translated into Danish, Russian, Chinese and Indian, to name just a few languages. We are clearly pleased to see this geographical spread, because we believe the issues we explored are relevant and increasingly pertinent everywhere. Normally you would pause a couple of years before you write the sequel... but frankly we have been bombarded by requests for more information – particularly information about real cases. This book will hopefully add to the armour you need as a brand to survive. **Survival** was the essence of our first book. **Winning and Succeeding** is the essence of this one.

We start by showing why becoming retail obsessed is the only way forward to ongoing business success at retail. Whether you're a conventional brand or a traditional retailer, the rules are the same. Why shouldn't they be? You are both in the business of selling. You are both retailers. You can both learn and grow. The precursor **RE**, for retail, should dominate your vocabulary, thinking and actions. How can everything you do become retail orientated? How can you have a RE point of difference?

From there we go on to show success in action. Having examined literally hundreds of case studies in the last three years, we have isolated 25 that we believe demand more attention – 25 case studies that show you some ways forward. Yes, you may know others and possibly better ones. But these 25 cases show clearly what can be done if you allow your brand to become retail obsessed and if you pursue a strategy for winning. We believe it's a very useful exercise to pause and reflect on their actions.

Finally we move towards the area of doing. We have put together an operational methodology that can be applied to your company – a template for action. That model will allow you to ask and review the questions you really need to ask to win. From there, you can develop and implement an actionable, relevant brand vision.

We're not pretending this book is a Pandora's box to success. We do, however, believe that by looking at new ideas, winning cases and operational tools you can get that little bit nearer. We hope every page gives you pause for thought, and a new idea. And sometimes it takes only a little to gain a lot. Go out there and win. Go out there and succeed. It's up to you. To succeed or not to succeed… that is the question.

Who can benefit?

Knowing how to succeed at retail is for anyone in any company who wants to increase the sales of their branded products. This will extend from the CEO to the brand manager to the salesman. The issues we explore are pertinent to all of them and increasingly relevant to their futures. Our experience to date has shown us that senior management has enormous interest in this area as it represents their most critical strategic issue, one that continues to grow in importance, one that needs a guide. The messages and lessons of this book are targeted at everyone in sales and marketing today, whether they be a brand manufacturer, retailer or communications agency. Whether they are directly involved or indirectly involved. Whether they are an assistant brand manager or the CEO. Whether they live and work in the United States, the UK, Scandinavia or China.

If you are interested in learning:

- Who are the world's best retail brands?
- How do you select winning brands?

- Is there a formula for success you can learn from?

you've come to just the right place! In *How to Succeed at Retail* you'll learn the key strategies you need to succeed and surpass your expectations... from the bottom up.

If you are like most people, chances are you are time crunched. You need answers in a concise, fast and easy-to-understand fashion. We know this and we understand the needs of the business entity, large and small alike. Whether a small brand, a big brand or a small or big retailer, we're here to tell you there is a formula for success... and you are just a few pages away from realizing it!

PS: howtosucceedatretail.com is an accompanying website which will allow you to access many more strategies, cases, tools and methodologies to help you succeed at retail even more. Additionally, you can download the operational methodologies in detailed PowerPoint charts, including all brainstorm exercises and instructions for execution. This methodology will be updated on a regular basis to keep you thinking! And doing!

Acknowledgements

Many people have contributed to this book. We would like to thank them all. But in particular we would like to thank the following people for their thoughts, direct help and guidance throughout. In no particular order:

C Migeul Brendl, PHD, Associate Professor of Marketing, INSEAD,
Martin West, CEO, Ashdown Group,
Bruce Vierck, Strategy Director, RTC Worldwide, Chicago,
Martin Lindstrom, Brand Futurist and author of *BRANDsense* and *BRANDchild*,
Roy Webster, Group Brand Manager, ASSA ABLOY Worldwide,
Magnus Von Reymond, Yale Retail Manager, ASSA ABLOY Worldwide,
Ulf Erlander, CEO, SWE, Stockholm,
Olle Hard, Partner, SWERETAIL, Stockholm,
Xavier Oliver, Chairman, BBDO, Spain,
Tom Watson, Worldwide Board Director, BBDO Worldwide,
Susan Froggatt, Sue Froggatt Training and Consulting,
Paul Freeman, s4p.com,
Michael Coye, Former EVP, Cordiant Europe,
Paul Lincoln, Chief Executive, National Heart Forum,
Chloe Lincoln, daughter and proof reader,
Kristina Eklund, Jens Lanvin and Mia Wahlstrom of Opinion Bengal, Stockholm,
Mathias Dittrich, Marketing Director of DLF, Sweden,
Egil Brathe of Movement.nu,
Mathias Segelman, CEO of RTV,
Helen Kogan, Jon Finch and everyone else at Kogan Page.

Thank you all.

Part 1

How to succeed by becoming REobsessed

It's only through becoming obsessed about something that we can motivate ourselves and others to succeed.

In our first book we talked in detail about how critical it is to become obsessed about retail when you run your business. We argued that only through becoming obsessed would you fully realize your true sales potential. We called that obsession RETAILIZATION. We argued that by retailizing your organization you would become truly retail-centric. By using the power of the definition of Retailization to full effect you could truly make a difference:

> Retailization: optimizing sale(s) by connecting brands to shoppers through the power of retail thinking.

We believe that one way of helping you to focus on this issue is to use the word retail wherever you can, or maybe more precisely the two letters RE wherever you can. You literally need to REtail every aspect of your business. REthink, REimagine and REstructure are three aspects of this that we described in our original book. Now we can take it further, into almost every other mindset you might encounter from REstorm to REsearch to RElearn. As we go through the next couple of hundred pages we will truly RE you to your core. Then hopefully you will succeed. And so will we!

1 REsolving the big squeeze

The squeeze goes on… and on

> If you can keep your head when all about are losing theirs… it's just possible you haven't grasped the situation.
>
> Jean Kerr – American humorist

The squeeze continues…

And continues and continues and continues.

In our first book we talked about the big squeeze that brands experience daily. We imagined a mountain of brands, a very big mountain of brands: a mountain so heavy and so dense that everything in it had been squeezed. It had been squeezed physically to a point where the individual brands had lost their form and identity. And right in the middle of this heap was your brand. That mountain is, of course, still here. Those squeezes, of course, never went away. They continue unabated. In fact their importance has continued to grow and grow. Why? Simply because the world continues to be squeezed. And the one thing that is particularly squeezed is brands. All the forces we described in our first book are there and more so than ever. Let's take them one by one and look more closely at the recent developments in those squeezes.

Retailer squeeze

The first squeeze we mentioned was, of course, retailer squeeze. We talked about a world where retailers were the new power. We talked about a world where the age of brands had been replaced by the age of retailers. The age of retailer power. That power certainly hasn't eroded. They simply continue to grow and grow and grow. The statistics prove it again and again. Just look at Wal-Mart with a current revenue of US \$330 billion and growing, or Tesco on the way to 33 per cent market share in the UK and growing and growing. Or ICA in Sweden topping 50 per cent market share! It's pretty much the same everywhere.

We like to think of this as a new phenomenon, but supermarkets or something like them first opened for business in the Peruvian Andes 4,000 years ago, if recent archaeological evidence is to be believed (*Daily Telegraph*, 2006b). An article in the journal *Nature* reported that a Smithsonian archaeological team had found evidence of an ancient trade in plant remains. Clearly Wal-Mart has been around longer than we thought! And it's moved well beyond the Andes! The squeeze started a lot earlier than anyone imagined! Of particular note is the rapid growth of the world's super-retailers' international businesses (Figure 1.1).

The retailers are increasingly the globalizers of today and tomorrow, not the brands (Figure 1.2). And retailers on a global scale are maybe what we're all going to have to become to survive! Brands need to become retail obsessed on a global scale because the world is becoming retail dominated on a global scale. Brands can no longer be mere suppliers – they must increasingly learn to sell direct themselves, on a global scale. The evidence is everywhere. Let's look at Wal-Mart yet again – a single retail entity that accounts for 35 per cent of the global sales of the world's top 10 grocery retailers. As of 31 January 2006, the company operated 1,209 discount stores, 1,980 supercenters, 567 SAM'S clubs, and 100 neighbourhood markets in the United States and internationally. It operated 11 units in Argentina, 295 in Brazil, 278 in Canada, 88 in Germany, 398 in Japan, 774 in Mexico, 54 in Puerto Rico, 16 in South Korea and 315 in the United Kingdom, as well as 56 stores through joint ventures in China. It employed 1.3 million people.

Then there's Tesco with their latest figures showing international growth at 23 per cent, online sales growth (whoever said online grocery was a failure never looked at Tesco in action) at 29 per cent and total employees at 400,000 (*Times*, 2006c). By the end of 2006 roughly 60 per cent of Tesco's floor space will be abroad, away from its UK base. Direct or

2006 – % share

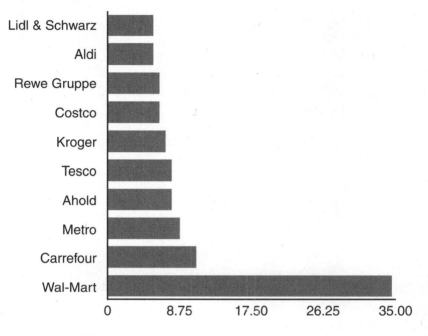

THE WORLD'S LARGEST GROCERS – % share of total
900 bn dollars combined turnover

Figure 1.1 Global grocers' share of the top 10
Source: IGD.com

joint venture operations now exist or are under negotiation in Korea, Thailand, Hungary, Poland, the Czech Republic, Slovakia, Japan, Turkey, Malaysia, China, India and the United States. That's an awful lot of the world's population. That makes it significantly more truly global than Wal-Mart, which is still essentially a US operation. Unlike Wal-Mart, Tesco is adapting to its markets. It is trying to be hypersensitive to its ultimate customers. Tesco is trying to prove Napoleon right when he described Britain as a nation of shopkeepers. In our view Tesco is the one to watch and it may yet become the world's biggest retailer. With 23 per cent international growth per annum it's not impossible to see it becoming as big as Wal-Mart. Some would argue it's actually better run – already! Each member of the Tesco board reportedly still spends a week per year stacking shelves and serving customers.

We used to live in a world where brand power was all, but slowly and inexorably brand power has been replaced by retail power. The retailers of

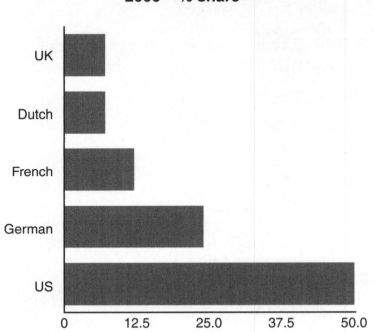

2006 – % share

THE WORLD'S LARGEST GROCERS BY NATIONALITY – % share
of total 900 bn dollars combined turnover

Figure 1.2   Global grocers' share by nationality
Source: IGD.com

the world are bigger, more dynamic and more in control than they have
ever been in their long history. Whether we like it or not, retail is at the core
of all our business decisions today, whether we're a mass retailer or a global
brand. And that core is increasingly global. While we talk about retailer
power, we also acknowledge that the reason it exists is simply because the
retailers have achieved exceptional growth in recent years, growth that
significantly exceeds the growth of the big branded companies. That
growth is particularly demonstrable internationally. Brands can learn from
understanding it better.

So why should we as brands globalize our retail efforts?

The reasons are just as relevant for retailers as for brands. These reasons
are simply the need for the consumer, scale, share and growth. Reasons
that can grow a small local Swedish clothes retailer called H&M into a

global force, for example. This global operation has been around since 1947. Hennes & Mauritz was founded in Sweden by Erling Persson, who was impressed with some of the US department stores back in the mid-1940s. Today you can find H&M in 22 countries – now that's global! Wal-Mart is only in 11. Sorry, 10... they just left Germany – after failing to understand and adapt to the Germans! Sorry, 9... they just left Korea – after failing to understand and adapt to the Koreans!

The first need is to **chase the consumer**, the ubiquitous global consumer who increasingly has more things that are similar than different. Mass communication has put us all on the same planet together, experiencing the same news, the same global trends and the same product, the same blogs and the same YouTubes! The desire for an iPod Shuffle from an Apple store to Nike sneakers to the latest gadget is a universal phenomenon. Shoppers and shopping have become the centre stage of people's lives the world over. Shopping is a social event... a lifestyle choice... a global choice. And the shoppers who shop at the global retailers expect the best products at the best prices. And an incredible choice at that! In France alone, between 1994 and 2003 the number of stock-keeping units (SKUs) in a hypermarket increased by more than 66 per cent to nearly 13,000 (Kapferer, 2006). In other words, in less than 10 years people were offered nearly 70 per cent more choices. Let's hope their brains expanded enough to deal with all those extra choices. The retailer of the future will have to meet that choice and be able to export it success-fully. You can increasingly see this phenomenon in the mass retailers who are offering more and more non-food products to their shoppers. Look at Wal-Mart, which entered the UK and helped transform ASDA into the second most successful mass-market retailer brand in the UK. It's even taking ASDA's famous own label clothes brand called George and turning it into a global brand in its own right in its stores worldwide. On Thanksgiving Day in 2005 there were more visitors to its website than to amazon.com – the first time that had ever happened. This probably explains why Amazon is planning to sell groceries online – the 34th product category it has entered! Wal-Mart now sells organic foods and Levi's (a brand specially made for them). It wants to sell more such things to middle-class America. Wal-Mart has worked hard to improve its image with new fashion brands, a trend-spotting office in Manhattan and fashion shows during New York's Fashion Week. The upgrading of its fashion is part of the company's larger campaign to expand into better quality, trendier merchandise. Wal-Mart, which has built its reputation on selling basics like socks and detergent, made a recent push into $2,000 flat-screen TVs and other trendy electronics, 600-thread-count sheets and organic foods (AP, 2006). The goal is to pry more money from the hands of its wealthier customers, diversifying beyond its core low-income shoppers, who are more vulnerable to economic downturns. However, its main competitive advantage remains its sheer efficiency. It is a suberbly lean machine (*Economist*, 2006a).

The second need often cited is **scale**: the bigger you are the more you can dictate to the suppliers of the world, whoever they may be. Retailers are using their scale advantages in the biggest market possible: the global market, through their sheer global scale (no real difference from brands and their ingredient suppliers). For example, Wal-Mart now is one of China's biggest customers, buying at least $15 billion of goods from China every year, accounting for 80 per cent of its imports into the United States. If Wal-Mart were a country, it would rank as China's eighth biggest trading partner, ahead of Russia and Britain! That's a lot of clout in potentially the world's biggest retail market. Wal-Mart was forecast (*Fortune* magazine, July 2005) to reach $3.2 trillion in sales by 2020, and to employ eight million people and occupy the land space of Las Vegas!

This scale can help with every facet of their business – in the United States 15 of the top megabrand advertising spenders are now retailers. In the first half of 2006 alone (adage.com, 2006), measured by millions of US dollars advertising spend, eight of the biggest spending brands are leading retailers in their own right:

1 Verizon $937.7
2 Cingular $628.6
3 Ford $540.3
4 AT&T $511.5
5 Sprint $496.0
6 Toyota $485.8
7 Chevrolet $443.0
8 McDonald's $379.5
9 Dell $336.4
10 Home Depot $306.9
11 Nissan $298.0
12 Honda $296.9
13 Vonage $293.2
14 T-Mobile $284.6
15 Target $279.1
16 Hyundai $268.2
17 Lowe's $243.7
18 Wal-Mart $233.5

19 American Express $229.6
20 Dodge $229.1

Arguably, because car makers are big retailers in their own right, we could make the number bigger by 8 to 16 out of 20! Look at your markets – you'll see the same pattern.

It's an interesting fact that most of today's global branded companies have major departments for dealing with major export nations. They seem to have forgotten that major global retailers are often bigger markets than their biggest export countries! Maybe we have our priorities a little mixed up. We were amused to hear anonymously of a major manufacturer who had asked its key retailers whether they were happy with the service they were supplying. Wal-Mart came back and informed them that they had to date that year received only 42 per cent of the goods they had ordered. The manufacturer didn't even know! But there again, they didn't have a system that feeds back global sales, store by store, every 15 minutes to their HQ in Bentonville.

Then there's the need for **share**. In a lot of markets the big mass retailers have frankly got too big – they have nowhere else to go. They are already starting to gain the attention of government bodies concerned with monopolies (particularly the European Union) and are increasingly coming under political influence. In France the big retailers have been recently 'asked' by the government to reduce their prices by 2 per cent to help the country control inflation! They're also increasingly finding it difficult to expand locally as planning permission becomes harder and harder to secure in the established countries. This fact alone has led to a major investigation commencing in the UK, where there is considerable concern as to the extent of land held and owned by mass retailers like Tesco in so-called 'land banks'. To be fair, the initial report did say that shoppers are enjoying better quality and prices that are 7 per cent lower than five years ago. However, it raised serious concerns about the planning regime that has allowed Tesco in Inverness to gain a 51 per cent share of the local market. In London, 85 per cent of the one-stop market is shared between Tesco and Sainsbury's alone.

According to *Fortune* magazine, the largest discount retailers are responsible for 80 per cent of the daily groceries sales in the United States – 10 years ago it was only 30 per cent. In the UK four chains have 75 per cent of the grocery market. In Sweden the major grocery retailers have more than 80 per cent of the market, with one of them exceeding 50 per cent share. The competition authorities in the UK please take note! The extreme example is Finland, where three retailers control a staggering 91 per cent of the mass fast-moving consumer goods (FMCG) market. Even in China, an embryonic Chinese retail market is already dominated by four major retailers, all Chinese. And now Wal-Mart and Tesco are entering with significant investments. With these sorts of shares it's pretty clear that they will have difficulty growing much bigger in their home markets. They must look outside.

Finally, there is **growth** itself per se. Retailers everywhere are under intense pressure – not only to compete and win, but also to keep winning, on and on. As competition increases, this becomes harder and harder. You have to keep on moving. You have to find fresh markets and leverage your global capabilities in them. Like a shark, once you stop swimming you sink!

In the search for growth, even India is under attack these days (*Economist*, 2006b). India's retail revolution is at last getting started. At the moment, 97 per cent of retail sales are made in more than 15 million tiny mom-and-pop stores. But now Reliance Industries, the country's largest business group, is to spend 250 billion rupees (US$5.5 billion) on big new shops over five years, starting on 3 November 2006, when it opened 11 convenience stores in the southern city of Hyderabad. And big foreign companies are moving in too. The government bans them from selling direct to individuals, but they have found a side door: starting wholesale and sourcing companies that supply a local retail partner. The first to do this was Australia's Woolworths, in league with Tata, India's second-largest firm. Tesco, from Britain, is expected to follow soon, and Wal-Mart and France's Carrefour are also thought to be searching for a way in.

The rise of retail globalization is inevitable as an ongoing trend. In 25 years' time, the high streets and shopping centres will be even more concentrated than they are now. The demands of consumers are forcing retailers to source better and offer lower prices. Economies of scale mean that larger chains are better able to cope with competitive pricing policies. The small guy is simply not able to do that today. These same economies allow new technologies to be used. Tesco recently said that the installation of thermal-imaging cameras in every store to count the number of customers had dramatically improved service, by cutting queues and making more checkout staff available. And even more importantly, boosting margins (*Times*, 2006b). Larger chains also deliver many other things that consumers demand, such as much greater convenience and fast reaction to trends. Retailers increasingly outperform brand manufacturers in terms of finding gaps in the market. Not only has their skill in interpreting shopper data improved, but retailers have much higher quality data in their hands.

Loyalty cards and in-store data have meant that retailers are now able to drive product categories themselves.

Tesco has, through the use of its loyalty card (14 million plus members) and scanning data information, divided its millions of customers into over 100,000 customer categories to better understand them, be they wine buyers or razor blade consumers. Or wine buyers who buy the best wine and the most razor blades. The shoppers' purchases define the categories and form an important base for direct communication with them. Buying behaviour is closely analysed and promotional campaigns adjusted accordingly. If we perceived a government to have such in-depth knowledge about us personally we would throw our hands up in horror. The power of this data is awesome. We heard of one retailer (anonymous) who had used scanning data from the leading brand in a particular category to identify the users' addresses through their credit cards. They were then mailed a joint retailer brand promotion for the number two brand in the sector. We think the number one brand wouldn't be too pleased!

We believe we haven't really seen the future global strength of retailers yet – their future power. People's hearts, minds and money will be controlled by the retailers of the future as they increasingly dictate the agenda, as they gain more control over the brands and dictate the patterns of choice according to their knowledge of us all. All of these forces point to the continuing and probably unstoppable globalization of retailers. They have grown constantly, developed their abilities and successfully understood their environments. They have improved execution in-store due to a better understanding of the shoppers and serviced them with increasingly better value propositions. But that hunt for value is at a cost – squeezed and struggling brands.

Shopper squeeze

The second squeeze we mentioned was shopper squeeze: the squeeze on brands exerted by our ever more sophisticated shoppers. Yet again there are examples everywhere you look of more and more sophisticated shopping techniques and methodologies that your average shopper is beginning to utilize on a daily basis. There are some countries that lead the way to shopping madness. The United States of America is often quoted as the most manic shopping country in the world. But the UK is catching up fast, with the publication of a new book called *The Shopaholic's Guide to Buying Online*, yet alone the recent best-selling book by Maggie Davis called *101 Things to Buy before You Die*. Somewhat sad we think.

Here's the book description:

> This shopping tour of a lifetime for women and men alights on the best of almost everything worldwide. Men can find the best place for bespoke suits; women will be guided to the top little black dress. Number One goodies include the most fabulous of accessories and grooming products. If you want to know where on the planet to locate the finest diamond ring, best olive oil, or motor scooter, you'll find the answer here. Items are sourced in American stores and/or international websites.

And then there is Russia! Where 88 billionaires and 50,000 millionaires are all in a buying frenzy (IHT, 2006d). Such frenzied buying is reflected in a Russian joke currently making the rounds. 'One wealthy businessman tells a friend of buying a tie for one hundred dollars! You fool, the other responds. You can get the same tie for 200 dollars just across the street.'

Where will it end? Clearly not in Moscow, where the average income in the city (by far the highest in Russia) is about $400 a month. Not that this stops Muscovites lining up to buy a $300 pair of shoes for $150 in popular end-of-season sales. At least a dozen shopping centres have opened during 2006 alone – large and small, in the centre of town and on the outskirts. They are expensive and very expensive. Every new mall generates instant crowds and traffic jams. Muscovites are buying ever more costly cars, with the very rich rushing to trade their Mercedes-Benzes and BMWs for truly prestigious cars. The day after the first Bentley dealership opened in February, all the new Continental GTs that were earmarked for Moscow had been spoken for – though the cars will not arrive for months. Prices start at €200,000, or about $260,000! Feeling poor?!

Clearly the cowboys in the film *Brokeback Mountain* got it all wrong... or did they!

> If you got nothing, you don't need nothing!
>
> Brokeback Mountain

Markets can be fundamentally changed by shopper power. Perhaps one of the most interesting of these is the art market, which is currently enjoying a boom. Until recently the art market was almost exclusively controlled by a few cliquey dealers and a few major auction houses. This was particularly so at the high end of the markets. But things changed quickly. eBay and

Artprice.com changed them. They change them by literally letting the shopper know the price of the product and making that product more accessible. Gone was the exclusivity of dealers who were the only people who seemed to know what was going on. Now everybody could buy through eBay and everyone could be an art expert via artprice.com. The latter was in fact the fastest-rising stock in the French stock market in 2005, approaching a 20,000 per cent increase. Clearly, knowing what shoppers want can be very profitable. The rise of the art market seems to have no end in sight at the moment, the biggest sale ever at Christies, New York, having been in November 2006, when a near 500 million dollars of sales were recorded, 200 million dollars more than anything that had ever happened before. Although they did say a similar thing in 1989, before the market collapsed.

And we're shopping more and more because the shops are open more and more. We're used to stories of Americans shopping 24 hours a day. But now it's becoming a truly global phenomenon. Across Europe, laws differ vastly. In Sweden and Britain many shops open on Sunday. Supermarkets already open 24 hours in the UK. In France shops can open on Sunday if they get court permission. A request for all shops to open on Sunday on the Champs Elysées is presently in the French courts for consideration. In Italy shops can open 13 hours a day until 10 pm. Now even Germany, which has long had draconian hours, is becoming more flexible. Berlin is leading the way by introducing 24-hour shopping, Monday through Saturday, and limited opening on some Sundays. So increasingly we can shop till we drop.

I went to the 24-hour grocery. When I got there, the guy was locking the front door. I said, 'hey, the sign says you're open 24 hours'. He said, 'yes, but not all at once'.

Blame it on the OFC

People who shop like crazy may apparently be slightly mad (*Sunday Times*, 2006a). A new scientific study from the United States shows that decisions about what to buy and what not to buy are made by a few neurons located in the orbitofrontal cortex (OFC) – an area of the brain just behind the eyes. People who shop like crazy may not be entirely normal and may indeed be slightly mad. Compulsive shoppers may have a dysfunction in a crucial decision-making area of their brain. And we thought they were just simple shopaholics. The study was subsequently published in *Nature*: 'We have long known that different neurons in various parts of the brain respond to separate attributes, such as quantity, colour and taste' (Camillo Padoa-Schioppa, the neurobiologist who led the study).

But quite how those different attributes are reconciled has been a mystery until now. You might, for example, like one shirt because it is blue, but another because of its material and another for its pattern. How do you choose between them or to buy any of them at all? To find out, Padoa-Schioppa and his colleagues studied the brain activity of macaque monkeys who were offered the choice between grapefruit juice and orange juice in differing quantities. The monkeys generally preferred grapefruit juice, but opted for orange juice under certain circumstances – if, for example, a sufficiently greater quantity was available. When three times more orange than grapefruit juice was offered, the monkeys switched their choice. Not stupid, these monkeys.

They found that while different areas of the brain are involved in taste, the decision to change the choice was made by only a few neurons in the OFC. Any small lesions or damage to that area could cause shoppers to behave irrationally. Padoa-Schioppa said: 'When you go to compulsive shopping, I think it is safe to assume that there is a dysfunction in the OFC which is leading to it.' Now we can truly understand the female compulsion to buy shoes. And the male compulsion to buy gadgets.

Such dysfunctions may be involved in other addictions as well. In various brain scans, when people gamble, we see the OFC light up. Similarly, drug addiction is a type of impulsive behaviour. 'I used to be buying something nearly every day, it's just this thing where I have to buy something. It's a force stronger than me. I can't control it' (Juliana De Angelis (*Sunday Times*, 2006a), a sales rep from West London).

One 20-year-old has been known to spend £15,000 ($28,000) in one weekend on shopping sprees in New York – Coleen McLoughlin, fiancée of the English footballer Wayne Rooney, who has become a national emblem of shopaholism. And let's not forget Michael Jackson, who pales even this into insignificance with his million-pound shopping sprees. The American Psychiatric Association has previously concluded that 'compulsive shopping' is not a specific mental disorder. Instead, some experts see it as an addiction associated with low self-esteem. The findings from Padoa-Schioppa's research may bring new light to the debate.

The discovery that the OFC is required to balance complex competing demands from different parts of the brain also resonates with a new survey that shoppers are being swamped by choice. Less than 1 per cent of a mass retailer accounts for 85 per cent of purchases. 'The odds of going to the store for a loaf of bread and coming out with ONLY a loaf of bread are three billion to one' (Erma Bombeck).

One in three would-be shoppers are so bamboozled by the range of goods on offer that they avoid large stores or leave without buying anything. According to an ICM poll in 2006, half of all customers over 65 said that the choice offered in supermarkets was 'overwhelming'. Tesco sells more than 50 types of bread roll and Waitrose nearly 50 types of sugar. How on earth do you choose between 50 types of bread roll!

> While generally consumers will say yes to more choice, if you keep adding to the range without managing it, it is a recipe for disaster.
> Richard Wildman of the business consultancy Accenture

One reason Marks & Spencer has improved its sales recently could be because it has reduced excessive choice. The latest US study also threw up another intriguing finding: when the monkeys were asked to choose between juices, their decision was not affected by the way the juice was offered. It did not matter in which order the juices were placed: the monkeys still made a calculated choice based on the values they had established. If there was at least three times more orange juice, they would choose orange whatever its position. Not stupid, these monkeys. 'This result has broad implications for possible psychological models of economic choice' (Padoa-Schioppa).

In other words, all that supposedly clever placing of certain items on high or low shelves, or near the front or back of shops, may not be as influential as retailers believe. Or at least as far as monkeys are concerned.

Private squeeze

The third squeeze is private label: in some ways, for some brands in some categories, the most formidable squeeze of all. Just look at recent reports on the impact of private label on communications, shoppers and retailer size.

> 'We get more and more demands to supply private label everyday. They give us all the specs, the formulations they want and the PRICE.'
> Recent quote from one of Europe's leading brands who wished to remain anonymous!

You won't find a CEO who sells in FMCG who doesn't see this as one of his major headaches. A headache he doesn't see a cure for. Just look at Procter & Gamble (P&G) in the United States and Costco. Here we see P&G, the biggest brand manufacturer in the world, deciding to do a special version of Tide, its leading detergent, just for Costco. It might of course have something to do with them delisting Pampers earlier. Deutsche Bank analyst William Schmitz was quoted as estimating that the change would cost P&G $150 million to $200 million a year, or up to 3 per cent of Pampers' total sales. Ouch!

Where retailer brands are present, they are either important (most of Western Europe), or growing (most of Eastern Europe), or both (Germany, Spain and the United States). The threat to manufacturer brands is huge in value terms – in some countries it represents more than one-third of the FMCG market. But in volume, and hence usage, it is even higher. Taking average retailer brand prices of 33 per cent below manufacturer brand prices equates to a volume usage share in some countries well above 50 per cent.

In other words, one out of two products in the basket could be private label.

In other words, one out of two choices could be private label.

In other words, brands compete in only half the market.

This data is further supported by independent data from DDB Brand Capital. Each of the five main European countries shows the same disturbing downward trend. When people were asked if they would stick to well-known brands, they universally recorded lower figures over recent years in the five major European countries – a very disturbing and consistent trend (Figure 1.3).

When we look at our own data from the International Nielsen Retailization survey, the trend is corroborated. When you ask shoppers whether they think private label is at least as good as a brand, private label is clearly gaining ground globally (Figure 1.4). They often wouldn't even change store if their favourite brands weren't present. With the increasing global shopper acceptance of private label, retailers need to worry less and less about brands.

But Retailer Brand success is not a law of nature. It varies significantly by country, category within country, retailer and shopper purchasing behaviour (diaper private label purchases increase by 50 per cent from first child to second child).

If you look at the food industry you can see how far private label has really penetrated (Figure 1.5). Would you want to be a milk brand or a soft drinks brand?

Private label is even reaching the shores of China (*FT*, 2006). Tesco is reported to be bringing its own brand of noodles to Chinese consumers as

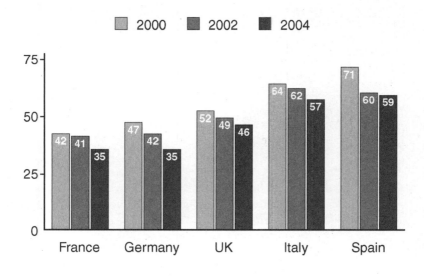

Figure 1.3　I try to stick to well-known brands (% people)
Source: DBB Brand Capital

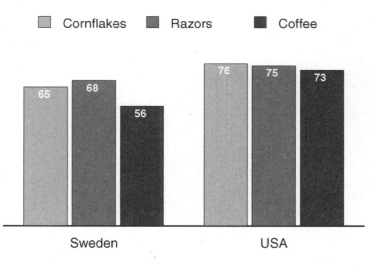

Figure 1.4　People who think private label is at least as good as a brand (%)
Source: International Nielsen Retailization Survey

part of their plans to launch up to 500 own-label 'value' products through its joint venture retail operation. As the British would say, talk about bringing coals to Newcastle. They are, after all, only following similar initiatives by Wal-Mart and Carrefour.

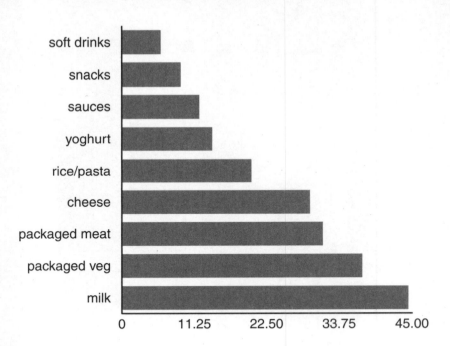

Figure 1.5 Private label global market share (%)
Source: A.C. Nielsen, J.P. Morgan

> Better quality pre-packaged products where the price is good... is a big area of opportunity.
>
> Ken Towel, Head of China for Tesco

One of the particularly alarming features of private label today is the price spectrum it covers. Look at Sainsbury's in the UK, which has very high levels of high-quality private labels. Here's a list of the prices for their orange juice products and brands. The brand Tropicana is the 'in-between' offering, sandwiched between private label offerings:

Sainsbury Pure Orange Juice	85 pence per litre
Original Tropicana	175 pence per litre
Sainsbury Freshly Squeezed Orange Juice with Bits	215 pence per litre

If you want to see more of the extent of this squeeze, look at Tesco's orange juice offerings (Figure 1.6). Spot the brand!

We've deliberately reduced the number of Tesco products for simplicity's sake – but let's say they easily outnumbered the brand offerings by five to

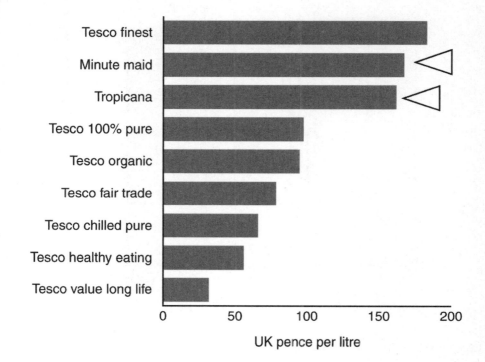

Figure 1.6   Tesco fruit juice offerings
Source: Jean-Noel Kapferer, HEC

one. Not only do Tesco and Sainsbury's have the cheapest and most expensive offerings, they have also limited the brands to a position as a mere benchmark – and a very squeezed one at that. STOP, you say, it couldn't happen here. Well, it could. These two UK retailers are arguably some of the world's best and frankly are 10 years ahead of their competitors abroad (including the United States). They are real tasters of what's to come – if you let it.

If we were a brand we would be feeling incredibly squeezed. We remember in the UK the days when you could get biscuits like Bourbon Creams, Custard Creams, Chocolate Chip Cookies and Ginger Snaps, all made by famous brands like Huntley and Palmers. Not only has that brand disappeared, but the products we mentioned are still available in Sainsbury's as a Sainsbury's brand only. Our brandless world grows ever closer. Clearly perception is changing and the real price difference between a brand and a private label is far in excess of the shoppers' perceived perception of the difference (Figure 1.7).

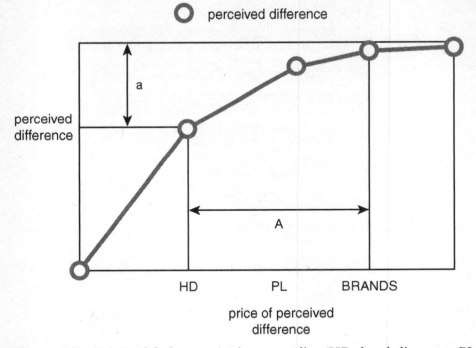

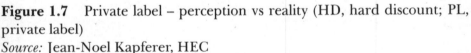

Figure 1.7   Private label – perception vs reality (HD, hard discount; PL, private label)
Source: Jean-Noel Kapferer, HEC

The real trouble with private labels is that they are a very different model from the one brands most shoppers understand. As Oliver Koll and Richard Herbert said recently at the ESOMAR Retail Conference, held in Budapest during April 2005, in a paper called 'Retailer brands – Heaven or hell, opportunity or threat':

> Private Labels are a major threat to manufacturer brands. Besides impressive growth rates the very nature of the Private Labels turns them into a different type of competitor: on the one hand, they are proprietary to the distribution partners manufacturers depend on. Therefore they cannot be dealt with in the same way as 'regular' competition. On the other hand, Private Labels typically use a very different business model (little R&D investment, little category-specific advertising, no cash expense for slotting allowances, etc.), which renders any benchmarking efforts against Private Labels difficult. Nonetheless, manufacturers need to better understand key success factors of Private Labels in order to stop their current growth patterns.

To help you understand those factors you need to go out there and answer some key questions.

HERE ARE A FEW QUESTIONS THAT NEED ANSWERING AS A PRIORITY? DO YOU KNOW THE ANSWERS? MAYBE YOU SHOULD?

Questions to your retailers

- Is private label becoming more important to your business?
- Is private label an important source of profit for you?
- Is your private-label business growing or not?
- Do you think private label is better or worse quality than it used to be?
- Do you think consumers think private label is worse or better quality than it used to be?
- Why do you think shoppers buy private label?
- Has the perception of what private label is changed over the years?
- Are you planning to increase the level of private label in the future?
- Do you believe there are any limitations as to what products can become private label?
- Do you see more and more premium-type private label products in the future?
- Is it possible to imagine a private label being more expensive than a brand?
- Do you think private label is as innovative as a brand in terms of its offer to the shopper?
- Do you see yourself promoting private label more in the future?
- Is it possible to imagine your store with private label products only?

Questions to your brands

- Is private label becoming a greater threat to your business?
- Is private label damaging your profitability?
- Do you think private label is better or worse quality than it used to be?
- Do you think consumers think private label is worse or better quality than it used to be?
- Why do you think shoppers buy private label?
- Has the perception of what private label is changed over the years?
- Do you manufacture private label or not?
- Is your private-label manufacture business growing or not?
- What is your main reason for manufacturing private label?
- Are you planning to increase the level of private-label manufacture in the future?
- What strategies do you think can help you win against private label?

- Do you believe there are any limitations as to what products can become private label?
- Do you see more and more premium-type private-label products in the future?
- Is it possible to imagine a private label being more expensive than a brand?
- Do you think private label is as innovative as a brand in terms of its offer to the shopper?
- Do you see yourself promoting private label more in the future?
- Is it possible to imagine a store with private label products only?

Questions to your shoppers

- Do you buy private label?
- How frequently?
- Is it good quality?
- Is it good quality for brands?
- Is it value for money?
- Do you believe there are any limitations as to what products can become private label?
- Do you see more and more premium-type private-label products in the future?
- Is it possible to imagine a private label being more expensive than a brand?
- Do you think private label is as innovative as a brand in terms of its offer to the shopper?
- Do you see yourself buying more private label in the future?
- Is it possible to imagine a store with private label products only?

If you knew the answers to these questions you would have better answers yourself. Ask yourself if you really do know.

Despite all this, there are signs of success. In one of the most concentrated retail markets of all – Sweden, brands are holding out. Look at a brand like Arla Foods, which has managed to keep private label at very low levels in the dairy industry to date, despite the fact that worldwide it is often 45+ per cent. Just look at a brand like Kavli (a maker of spreads in tubes), which continues to grow its market share in almost every sector it's in. How? Many things, but one thing above all. Clever use of their shelves. Their brand really does stand out. Not rocket science, but little things like making sure their tubes are placed in straw baskets above the fish they garnish; ensuring usage is linked to consumption.

One final word though… and then along came TERTIARY BRANDS (Figure 1.8)! What are we talking about? This is a new UK phenomenon

where we are now getting own-label brands that have no label. No manufacturer brand label. No retailer brand label. This is particularly used in
commodity-orientated sectors like meats where heavy discounting is the
norm. The farmers lambast them as 'flags of convenience' (*Grocer*, 2006).
We can see the future now and it certainly looks squeezed to us.

Media squeeze

The final squeeze is media and this squeeze continues with a frenzy. 'We
have moved from mass production and mass marketing to mass participation' (Charles Leadbeater's speech at the ESOMAR's Congress in
London, 2006).

We might have said we have moved from mass production and mass
marketing to mass channel. Mass channel is where mass participation takes
place. Retail is the point of action.

> It's clear we need new channels to reach consumers. Brands that rely too
> heavily on mainstream media, or that are not exploring new technologies
> and connection points, will lose touch.
>
> Jim Stengel, global marketing officer, P&G.

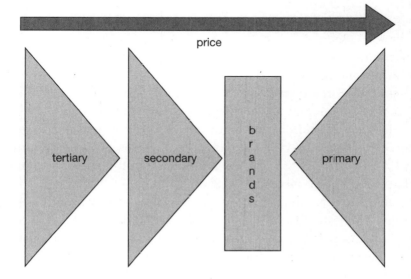

Figure 1.8   The future private label spectrum

A new study on media proliferation does not make cheerful reading for the United States' (or anyone else's) conventional TV broadcasters (McKinsey, 2006). It argues that by 2010, traditional TV advertising will be only one-third as effective as it was in 1990. Not bad in 20 years! This is due to an assumed 15 per cent decrease in buying power triggered by cost-per-thousand rate increases, a 23 per cent decline in ads viewed owing to watchers literally switching off, a 9 per cent loss of ad engagement caused by increases in multitasking and a 37 per cent saturation-induced reduction in message impact.

But there's more! 'You've also got pronounced changes in consumer behaviour while they're consuming media,' warns McKinsey director Tom French. 'And ad spending is decreasingly reflecting consumer behaviour.'

In other words, it isn't working the way it used to! That's partly because the net has taken over as our prime source of viewing. Broadband reached nearly 220 million subscribers worldwide in 2005. The funny thing is we spend more than ever on conventional broadcasting! In real terms, ad spending on primetime broadcast TV has increased over the last decade by about 40 per cent – despite a fall in viewing levels of almost 50 per cent. Paying more for less obviously creates a significantly higher cost-per-viewer-reached, a trend also reflected in radio and print. Many technological factors have contributed to these changes over the past 16 years – and will continue to do so at an accelerated rate over the next few years. Among the historical influences on TV viewing are cable, PCs, cellphones, CD players, VCRs, game consoles and the internet. More recent – and future – determinants are PDAs, broadband internet, digital cable, home wireless networks, MP3 players, DVRs and video-on-demand.

Forrester Research's most recent North American Consumer Technology Adoption Study shows people in the 18–26 age group spending more time online than watching TV. The same is true in the UK, where similar measures have suggested similar behaviour. In the UK alone the average Brit spends 23 hours a week surfing – ie one day in seven! People are adopting new technology faster than ever before, making them more receptive to advertising via blogs, podcasts and web-cellphones (Figure 1.9).

Frankly, the only thing saving conventional communications is the simple fact that there's no room! (Ad Age, 2006).

And then there's the producers – the people who produce the content that goes with our ads. 'PAIN is temporary, film is forever' (*Economist*, 2006c). That hopeful thought, which found its way into the original script of Peter Jackson's recent remake of *King Kong*, would be welcomed by today's increasingly besieged entertainment industry. Media companies are suffering to an extent they haven't seen before. In the United States, shares

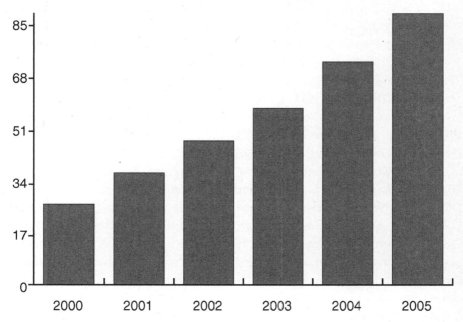

E-commerce retail sales ($bn)

Figure 1.9 The net never really stopped growing
Source: Fortune

of 'old' media firms such as News Corporation, Comcast and other giants of television, film, radio and print have fallen 25 per cent behind the Industrial S&P 500 in the past two years. On the other side, the market value of Google, which made its debut on the stock market in 2004, is now equal to the combined worth of Walt Disney, News Corporation and Viacom, three giants of the old media empire.

> The market thinks something's going to get them, whether it's piracy, personal video recorders, or Google.
> One investor, who recently moved two-thirds of his $1 billion fund out of American media

Desperate to rescue its share price, Viacom broke itself in two on 3 January 2006. Time Warner, the biggest media group of all, is under attack from Carl Icahn, the renowned corporate splitter. The big groups have seen their newspapers and magazines lose readers and advertising to the internet; their music businesses suffer piracy and falling sales; and someone else's video games captivate new generations of consumers. Yet, if Hollywood teaches one thing, it is that stories can be remade and dreams can come true. In the same way as big retailers, including Wal-Mart and Tesco, have discovered advantages online, so too will big media companies. The heroine could be saved yet.

Other major changes are on the way

Wal-Mart Stores, Microsoft, Hewlett-Packard, Philips Electronics, Home Depot and Toyota-owned luxury auto marque Lexus have banded together to pilot a revolutionary new scheme that will buy TV airtime via a special auction facility on eBay. Its sponsors have committed $50 million (€39M; £25M) to the embryo system, named eMedia Exchange, which is scheduled to launch in early 2007. Now the retailer has become the media controller.

A new free website called mysupermarket.co.uk allows consumers to compare the price of their virtual shopping trolley at the major retailers and alerts them to cheaper alternative items and money-saving offers. They claim that the typical online shopper could save 20 per cent on their weekly bill and still get the same quality. Now the shopper truly is in charge.

And you all seem aware of the squeeze.

We run retailization workshops and presentations around the world and one question we always ask is: rank your priority in terms of the squeezes you encounter. Although there are some exceptions, the vast overall consensus is clear:

1. Retailer power.
2. Shopper power.
3. Private label.
4. Media changes.

Despite this forced ranking, they're all seen as major issues facing the brands of today, whether you're selling jam or Sony PlayStations.

2 REflating the brand

So have people succeeded in fighting the squeezes? Ever wondered about those people who spend a fortune on a small bottle of Evian water? Try spelling Evian backwards...

The answer is yes and we see examples everywhere of brands coming up with ingenious ways to better compete in the age of the retailer. We will show these in detail later. Brands simply have to pump themselves up and in effect REflate their very essences. Fortunately there's hope!

Brands need retailers and retailers need brands! Who first said that? A retailer or a brand manufacturer? We don't think we need to investigate this issue a lot. The reality, whether they admit it or not, is that most brands today feel that retailers only need them as a comparison to show the world that their own retailer label is a better buy than the old-fashioned brand. During most of the last century it was quite clear that the retailers could not live without the strong brands, and it was equally clear that consumers couldn't live without the strong brands either. Unfortunately for brands, the world has changed. When brands as strong as Kellogg's or Ariel can be delisted at the whim of a buyer and lose more than 30 per cent of the Scandinavian market overnight, or Pampers in the United States is thrown out of Costco, it is evident that brand power has been replaced by retail power. Pampers, Kellogg's and Ariel were strong enough to survive the squeeze and return to the shelves, but what happens to smaller brands in such a competitive and restrictive environment? Companies need to sell, but are they being allowed to? The retailers of the world are getting bigger and bigger and are now experiencing the same criticism that many multi-national companies experienced in the 90s.

To be fair, all they have done is to focus on satisfying their customers' needs, developing their formats and rationalizing their businesses. It is understandable that some of them feel that it is somewhat unfair that they are criticized for doing a good job for their customers and for their shareholders. Don't people and governments want cheap prices and lower inflation? Many people in the UK believe that the authorities need to control the further expansion of Tesco, Sainsbury's and ASDA, but is this really desirable? Wouldn't it be better to encourage the FMCG companies to get their act together and start doing what they used to be good at, developing superior products and creating proper cooperation or co-opetition with the retailers?

Everything has to be looked at in its true perspective. The retail concentration looks extreme in the UK, with a Tesco market share of more than 31 per cent, but that situation is nothing compared to the extreme situation in Finland, where three supermarket chains control a staggering 91 per cent of the mass FMCG market. The Finnish situation looks out of control when seen from a UK perspective, but is actually OK when seen from a Finnish one, albeit it is somewhat dull for the shopper.

Figure 2.1 contains a small list of why brands and retailers should be helping each other. We're sure you could make this list even longer. When you look at these very different offerings, you wonder why a war seems to be going on. But there again, you could say that about most wars. Their reasons for being are often completely illogical. This is clearly the case here.

BRANDS NEED RETAILERS	RETAILERS NEED BRANDS
distribution	image
selling power	choice
competitive context	innovation
promotion	margin
growth	growth
shopper knowledge	consumer knowledge

Figure 2.1 We need each other

Co-opetition is the way forward

P&G, the world's biggest branded company, keeps a permanent staff of 200 at Bentonville, the Wal-Mart HQ in Arkansas, United States.

In most modern business theories, competition is seen as one of the key forces that keeps firms lean, drives innovation and ensures happy consumers. However, increasingly co-opetition is seen as the way forward, defined as cooperation with suppliers, customers and firms producing complementary or related products that can lead to expansion of the market and the formation of new business relationships, perhaps even the creation of new forms of enterprise. The theory of co-opetition is particularly relevant in the era of retail power. The definition of retail co-opetition is just as relevant. Simply put, it is the cooperation between retailers and manufacturers that will jointly grow the essence and business of both partners while stimulating the category as a whole. There is little doubt that the big retailers will continue to grow, but it is equally clear that it will be increasingly difficult for them to grow their home market shares much more. Even shoppers will turn against them if they become too big.

Think of Formula One, a few years ago. Nearly everybody loved Michael Schumacher and Ferrari, but when Schumacher started winning all the races, the industry started discussing if it was time for the Formula One rules to be changed. Sound familiar? – Tesco and the Monopolies Commission. All Ferrari had done was to follow the existing rules, train and trim their set-up, down to the smallest detail. They had done everything right to become number 1. Retailers have also done a lot of things right to get where they are today. But they must remember where they are good and where they are bad – where their real strengths are, where their real weaknesses are.

Use REinvention as the trigger for co-opetition

Retailers are fantastic at selling things, but very few retailers are very good at developing things. That used to be the raison d'être of the brands. But with their obsession for volume they have often mixed up genuine innovations with the next flavour-extension or volume-variant package. Many FMCG companies have forgotten what originally made them big. When it comes to the retail arena, shoppers reach out for products, but they are often disappointed. Lots of companies have a brand these days, but few have a product. Or as Sir Martin Sorrel puts it: 'We have become so obsessed with the sizzle that we have forgotten the steak'. The brand is never the solution. The product is. In their book *Blue Ocean Strategy*, authors W Chan Kim and Renee Mauborgne researched the effect of creating groundbreaking, creative new products, rather than variations of already existing products. Their conclusion was that 86 per cent of new product launches were variants of existing products and accounted for 39 per cent of total profit. The remaining 14 per cent of new products were real new products and accounted for a massive 61 per cent of total profit. Real products mean real profit.

The most successful grower of brands in the mass markets is arguably Procter & Gamble. P&G has built the biggest brand business in the world by understanding its competitive context better than anybody else. Its key to growth has been to constantly out-innovate not only the competition, but also itself. P&G's finest ability is to make continuous improvements to its brands through a constant series of innovations, adding small additional fighting features to its armoury, and sometimes creating entirely new product ideas and categories.

> Product innovation has been the cornerstone of our success in the past and it's the primary strategy for success in the future.
>
> pg.com

They have constantly sought to win each given shelf in each given market they operate in. Among other things, their innovations have been driven by the need to compete with and understand outstanding competitors and find ways to beat them. It is this drive for constantly out-innovating competitors that defines P&G as a company. Incremental never-ending change is the name of the game, and staying one step ahead is P&G's yardstick of measurement, and a very successful strategy it has been. P&G has over 16 brands exceeding sales of US $1 billion each, and is the global leader in four core product categories: fabric and home care, beauty care, baby and family care, and health care. P&G have used this innovation to good effect when creating word-of-mouth marketing. Their site Tremor.com lets teenagers be directly involved in product development and sampling. Hundreds of thousands of teenagers have used this site and their word of mouth is capable of reaching epidemic proportions, directly to key target audiences like friends and family.

We should strive to be invited into consumers' lives and homes.
Jim Stengel. Global Marketing Officer, P&G

Other big brand builders like Gillette have followed the same pattern for years. Gillette, like P&G, understands that product innovation must be constant, with noticeable (or at least marketable) improvements year in, year out. In today's market a company cannot count on consumer loyalty, and instead must constantly 'sell' the customer on product value. The Sensor was launched in 1990 and was the first major new product introduced by Gillette for 25 years. When BIC disposables threatened to turn the market into a cheap commodity one, Gillette responded with this apparently new shaving experience. There was initially only one blade and one lubrastrip, but step by step, blades and lubrastrips and more and more floating heads were added to produce what the company would like customers to perceive as the ultimate shave. Constant innovation has kept Gillette comfortably ahead of the competition – from Mach 3 to Mach 3 Turbo to M3 Power to Fusion. The incremental innovations from Gillette have kept the brand securely positioned as the global leader. The brand still maintains a 70-plus per cent global market share and quickly gains market leadership with every new product launch, a remarkably unique performance for such a high-consumption, everyday-use product. It has understood its competition from the very beginning and has always kept one step ahead.

Metro International is another successful example of how to out-innovate. In a world of free-flowing information and news on the internet, many newspaper businesses have been challenged. Tabloids have had an especially rough time. Because of the faster, more superficial and less quality-concerned nature of the tabloid product, readers more easily switched to the internet without feeling a large loss of quality. As a result, many tabloids have experienced a drop in sales and therefore a drop in advertising revenues, an evil circle that nobody seemed to be able to break – that is, until Metro International arrived on the scene with a radical new proposition, through out-innovating the competition in terms of pricing and distribution. It started giving its newspapers away for free on the streets and on public transport, something it could afford to subsidize through paid advertising. The first *Metro* newspaper was published in Stockholm in 1995. Now, there are 58 editions in Europe and international launches in 2006 include Bohemia, Moravia, Castellon, Canary Islands, the Basque country, Mexico City and Croatia (Mandmeurope.com, 2006). According to the Metro website, the free daily is the largest and fastest-growing international newspaper in the world. Seventy daily *Metro* editions are published in over 100 major cities in 21 countries in 19 languages across Europe, North and South America, and Asia. It's also now official! *Metro*, the flagship title of Metro International, has been declared the 'World's Largest Global Newspaper' by no less an authority than Guinness World Records.

You can see the effect of innovation in the FMCG world, where the rate of innovation is clearly closely correlated with the share of private label in that category (Figure 2.2). This argument can be taken even further when you start to think how brands should really innovate in practice. Figure 2.3 shows where the real opportunities lie for most brands in rebuilding volume by giving more for less and/or building true value innovations by providing shoppers with far more for more. How does your new product development (NPD) programme stack up to this? The former is really a defence policy. The latter – pure attack. The only way you can truly make your brand consistently innovative is to offer far more for more. When you look at your own products innovations, do you really meet this objective?

Or are you just producing line extensions and calling them innovations? As the head of a major Scandinavian retailer recently said to us: 'I'm sick of brands coming here and saying they've been in the business for a hundred years and know everything there is to know. Here's our new line extension flavour variant. Give us more shelf space. I don't want this. I want innovation. I want food iPods.'

Yes, product development is difficult, but it is one of the most important ways for a brand to keep its position at retail level, and one of the only really consistent ways to avoid private label competition. Food brands in particular should be embracing the leading trends like health, food labelling and the environment and using them to distance themselves from the retailer brands. As Figure 2.4 shows, there are plenty of opportunities out there.

You only need to think about Gillette or iPod or Persil. The future belongs to retailers and brands that proactively create wants – retailers and brands that are transforming boring consumption situations into highly motivating shopping experiences.

Shopping for your brand is as important as your brand. There is no doubt that brands need retailers and that retailers need brands, but retailers only need strong brands (as brands need strong retailers) – brands that understand the new retail world; brands that understand that the product is key; that they have to build their brands, not only from mass media, but also from the shelf. Innovation is and always has been the key.

You need to make this innovation work for you as a cooperative tool with retailers. Remember the Scandinavian retailer. It's the one real edge that's

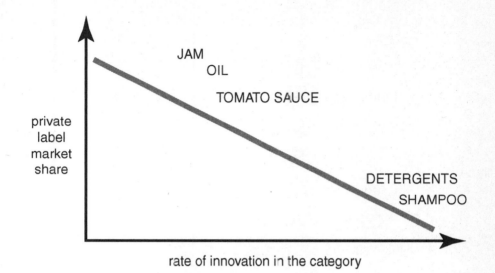

Figure 2.2   Innovation is the best defence
Source: Jean-Noel Kapferer, HEC

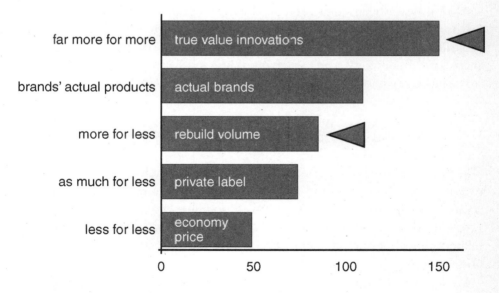

Figure 2.3   Innovation is the catalyst
Source: Jean-Noel Kapferer, HEC

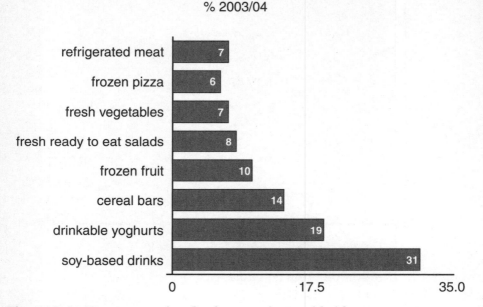

Figure 2.4   Fastest-growing food categories worldwide
Source: A.C. Nielsen

yours. But it's an edge that's under threat. As global retailers grow ever bigger and more international they have more and more opportunities to source those innovations from anywhere and anyone. Logistics cost-wise, the world has never been smaller. It is as cheap to source from China and Eastern Europe these days as from Spain to France or Normandy to the Riviera. Anything can be copied, and copied very quickly these days – even and especially food. Being local won't save you. Being innovative just might. So make sure your innovations are real. And big! And constantly REinvented!!

Co-create the co-opetition

One final word on co-opetition. Brands should use their creativity as a force to encourage co-opetition. They should arrange creative sessions with retailers where together they creatively explore the category and what's possible: what's possible in terms of innovation, what's possible in terms of promotion, what's possible in terms of joint efforts, what's possible in terms of category-growing cooperation.

When something is new and improved – which is it? If it's new, then there has never been anything before it. If it's an improvement, then there must have been something before it!

3 REassessing the shopper

RE-me

We talked in our first book about the need to start thinking shopper, shopper, shopper. Those shoppers are in charge to an extent they have never been before.

> It's a consumer revolution – a demanding but liberating shift. The rise of this powerful consumer boss marks one of the most important milestones in the history of branding.
>
> A G Lafley, CEO P&G, *Advertising Age*, 75th anniversary edition

We need to reappraise our shoppers and get to grips with what's really driving them to consumption. Are you truly near or far from your shopper (Figure 3.1)? Do you truly research and understand what motivates them? Are you in the bottom left-hand quadrant or the top right? And even more importantly, where's your competition?

Part of that reappraisal starts with understanding the 'me shopper' of today (IHT, 2006b). The world (arguably unfortunately) has become 'It's all about me'. A **RE-me** world as we call it. Just look at the mountains of new products and services, from vanity film making to personalized perfumes. Companies have found ways to make big money from catering to customers' needs to see themselves, and only themselves, in what they buy.

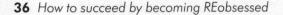

> Customers set their own rules.
>
> Michael Dell, Chairman of Dell

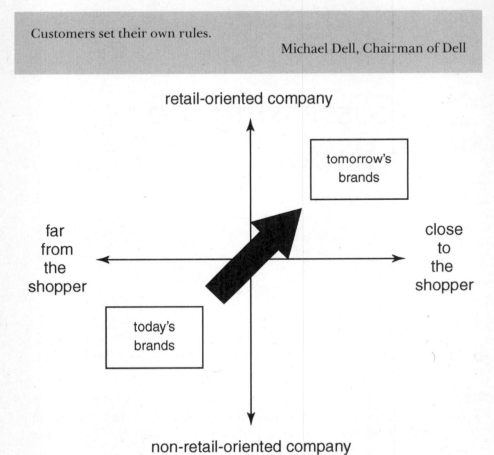

Figure 3.1 Retail orientation grid

And whether it's a tiny bookshop or the world's largest maker of mobile phones, both small and large companies are getting in on the act – integrating 'me'-centred products into their sales lines and 'me'-directed approaches into their marketing and selling strategies.

More than marketing, though, the 'me' business is a direct result of advances in manufacturing technology that have turned the traditional economies upside down, allowing companies to turn out small batches of products – or just a single product – at a lower, more efficient cost.

The signs are everywhere:

- Watch Me, a line of flashlights.
- Personal care products like Envy Me body lotion by Gucci.
- Color Me frosted nail polish by Avon.

- Anya Hindmarch, a maker of expensive handbags in London, will plaster a customer's image on a bag as part of her company's luxury 'Be a Bag' service.
- Just Me Fragrance for women by Paris Hilton.
- A Denver-based company, My Twinn, a subsidiary of the internet merchant eToys Direct, will fashion a 23-inch, or 58-centimetre, doll designed to look like the person you are giving it to – complete with similar hair and eye colouring – for about $139.

> What consumers really appear to hunger for are products that fit their unique needs, wants and desires. They want products that talk just to them, work just for them and appeal just to them on an emotional level.
> Tom Vierhile, executive editor of the trend-tracking Productscan

Vierhile said it was clear that marketers had recognized this as a trend with staying power and that they were trying harder to make a personal connection with their customers. In 2004, Productscan Online found that 56 new products in North America had incorporated the word 'me' into their names. That's up from 14 in 1999. Names like these 'would have been dismissed as overly narcissistic a decade or two ago', Vierhile said. 'But today's consumers aren't shy about spending money on themselves.'

It seems 'just for me' marketing is what consumers want. In a study conducted in late 2004, Productscan Online found that more than one-third of all European and American consumers felt that it was either important or very important to differentiate themselves from others by what they buy and what they use. Clearly we all want to be different. This drive for an increased desire for self-expression and for standing out is being directly driven by the leading social trends, which tend to lead to a focusing on ourselves and on our own needs rather than on someone else:

- sizable increases in people living alone;
- marrying later;
- higher divorce rates;
- overall ageing of the population;
- higher personal disposable income;
- people living for today, rather than tomorrow.

Of course, a focus on self is not a new phenomenon. The 1980s were widely known as the 'me decade', a period of a focus on self-improvement, conformism and consumerism in reaction to the social upheaval of the 1970s. Remember Michael Douglas and his famous quote in the film *Wall Street*: 'greed is good'? The embodiment of the era was the yuppie or young urban professional – typically a single young city dweller who earned a high income at a demanding white-collar job and filled the remaining hours with shopping for luxury goods, dining in restaurants and working out at the gym. Boy, things haven't changed! This time, however, industry analysts say, there is no overarching group, like the yuppies, that comprises the self-seekers; each individual wants to be, well, individual. In other words, there are more yuppies than ever. We just don't call them that.

> Looking back on it now, everybody viewed the 90s as being a very aware decade, but it was actually deeply boring; everything was beige, and politicians were trying to agree with everyone else. But now we're moving back towards a period of dissent, and so more opinions are being expressed, and more individuality is coming out – whether in regard to Iraq or in regard to shopping.
>
> Chris Sanderson, co-founder of the Future Laboratory,
> a forecasting and research group in London

The trend has created something of a challenge for packaged goods marketers, since 'just for me' marketing is the antithesis of the way packaged goods have traditionally been marketed, with an emphasis on low-cost, mass-produced items. And, of course, selling them is in itself that much more difficult.

Combine these attitudes with the recent advances in personal technology, and it is no surprise that there are higher consumer expectations for more 'me'-type products.

> The internet and technology in general had helped spur creativity, individuality and customization in the marketplace. This trend has been helped by our ability as individuals to increasingly personalize all the technology we come into contact with, whether it be the MP3 player or just your mobile phone.
>
> Sanderson of the Future Laboratory

High-speed internet has been transformed into a mouthpiece for the world, as the spread of broadband unleashes a swell of ventures designed to celebrate an individual's tastes and desires.

For example, growing in popularity are so-called MP3 blogs that allow anyone with a computer and an internet connection to hunt down and post their favourite musical snippets on the internet for others to discuss and download. And who leads the world in blogs? The French, of course (Figure 3.2). Make sure your retail strategy in France takes it into account. More people, too, are posting videos of their friends and family on the internet. A flourishing offshoot of blogging, or the creating of an online web diary, is video blogging, or vlogging.

Thousands of people are now taking their own digital videos and posting them on the web. You can get a glimpse of how wide-ranging vlogging has become by checking out an online directory at www.vlogdir.com.

> Mass personalization – a seeming oxymoron – is the next big thing in the technology market.
>
> Rob Enderle, principal analyst at Enderle Group,
> a technology research concern in California

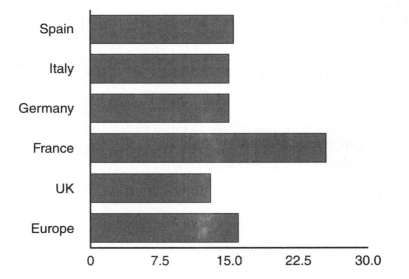

Figure 3.2 Readers of blogs on the internet by country (%)
Source: Ipsos MORI

Nokia, the world's biggest maker of cellphones, has helped lead the charge in the transformation of the phones from simple calling devices to personalized accessories. Nokia was early to offer customers the ability to customize their cellphone keyboards with interchangeable coloured plastic covers, as well as the ability to personalize ring tones by either composing their own or creating them from a favourite CD. The personalization of cellphones is a driving force in the self-identity phenomenon and it shows little sign of stopping – the ring tone market in Western Europe, now estimated at close to €1.4 billion, or $1.7 billion, in sales per year, could reach €2.2 billion in annual sales by 2008.

Today, there is a burgeoning industry of service providers building businesses around customizing laptops and iPods. To a certain extent, the trend towards hyper-personalization was about feeding people's egos and allowing them to enjoy a certain exclusivity. Retailers are tapping into the trend by offering invitation-only sales to build customer loyalty.

This 'me' trend has legs. It makes money for industries that are finding their traditional sources of revenue eroded by new business models and is driving a lot of revenue into a large number of markets. Companies and retailers that recognize and embrace the 'me' trend are likely to benefit from it. Just look at Kodak and its EasyShare Gallery, which allows consumers to view, store and share photos on the web. Kodak, like all camera and film companies, is only just now coping with the rapid shift to digital photography. It may yet save the company from its past.

Mass market to mass of niches

The internet is displaying a key trend that backs up this movement to the 'me' culture for the future. In short, although we still obsess over the leading brands, they are not the economic force they used to be. Where are our fickle shoppers going? No single place.

They are scattered to the winds as markets fragment into countless niches (Figure 3.3). Increasingly the mass market is turning into a mass of niches. The rise of the tail is explained further in a new book, *The Long Tail – How Endless Choice is Creating Unlimited Demand*, by Chris Anderson. As he puts it very succinctly: Endless choice is creating Unlimited demand.

It's just a matter of meeting that demand. More later. Are your retail efforts geared up to meeting those long tails? Can you produce niche products for individual customers? Do you present yourself as a brand that caters for RE-me?

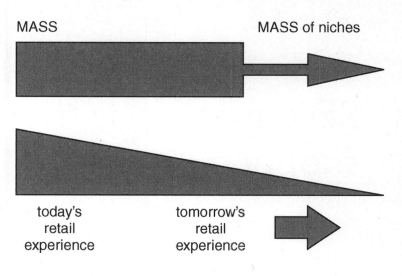

MASS   MASS of niches

today's   tomorrow's
retail   retail
experience   experience

Figure 3.3   The long retail tail

4 REconnecting to the shopper

Tesco is so powerful that it can introduce virtually any product or service in the UK and have an instant hit. When it launched its Tesco Mobile service, for example, it attracted 500,000 customers in less than 14 months. How? They're incredibly knowledgeable and close to their customers:

- Tesco pays 1 per cent in dividends to its customers – over one billion pounds.
- Tesco has 14 million Tesco cards in circulation.
- Many Tesco stores open 24 hours.
- One-stop Tesco stores have dramatically changed the UK retail scene.
- Tesco sells the cheapest gasoline in the UK to their customers – always a good reason to go there.

You need to get closer to your shopper and maybe one way of doing this is to start listening to them and start cooperating with them. You need to start 'listening to shoppers' more. Too many focus groups have their predetermined questionnaires which moderators are determined to get through, whatever it takes. This is not conducive to good research, which should be relaxed and stimulating at the same time. We should not treat shoppers as laboratory rats and we should avoid processes that provide average statistics. Average statistics give you average results. Throw away glass research mirrors and talk to shoppers about their lives and their shopping experiences – not just products. You might be surprised by what you hear.

By listening to people more effectively we get closer to the true shopping nature of brands. Brands are living entities. Brands are holistic. Brands are not about stereotypes. Brands are about paradoxes. Brands are about talking to everyone. Brands are about emotions.

To listen, we need to slow down...

The famed editor Maxwell Perkins (1884–1947), who helped make Ernest Hemingway famous, decided to test his hypothesis that no one really listens to what others say at most social events. Arriving late to a cocktail party, Perkins grasped his hostess's hand and said, 'I'm sorry I'm late but it took me longer to strangle my aunt than I had expected.' 'Oh, I completely understand,' said the hostess, smiling sweetly. 'I'm so happy you could come.'

To ensure we listen properly we need to separate our obsessions about creating brand fantasies from the realities of operating a brand in a pragmatic real retail environment (Figure 4.1). Yes, the two are linked – but they're not the same.

Springwise have taken this one stage further and come up with the concept of customer-made. Springwise.com is a database of leading trends which we highly recommend you tap into on a regular basis.

> CUSTOMER-MADE: 'The phenomenon of corporations creating goods, services and experiences in close cooperation with experienced and creative consumers, tapping into their intellectual capital, and in exchange giving them a direct say in (and rewarding them for) what actually gets produced, manufactured, developed, designed, serviced, or processed.'

We think this is an excellent thought when it comes to talking to your shoppers. Maybe it should be renamed SHOPPER-MADE. When did you last talk to them? If at all. When did you last actively develop a product with a shopper in mind?

They argue that customers (ie shoppers) are motivated by five things when it comes to helping companies develop their products:

- Status: people love to be seen, love to show off their creative skills and thinking.

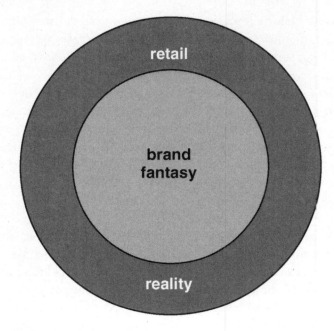

Figure 4.1 Reality vs fantasy

- Bespoke lifestyle: something consumers have been personally involved in should guarantee goods, services and experiences that are tailored to their needs.
- Cold hard cash: getting a well-deserved reward or even a profit cut for helping a company develop The Next Big Thing is irresistible.
- Employment: in an almost ironic twist, CUSTOMER-MADE is turning out to be a great vehicle for finding employment, as it helps companies recruit their next in-house designer, guerrilla advertising agency or brilliant strategist.
- Fun and involvement: there's pleasure and satisfaction to be derived from making and creating, especially if co-creating with brands one loves, likes or at least feels empathy for.

Here are a few examples of the ways customers have been helping.

- Virtually every brand these days seems to be inviting their customers to contribute to their next advertising campaign: L'Oreal's You Make The Commercial, FireFox's Flicks, MasterCard's Write a Priceless Ad, JetBlue's Travel Stories and McDonald's Global Casting.
- Buzz advertising was started last year in Luxembourg. It specializes in word-of-mouth marketing campaigns waged from blog to blog. It has

worked with brands like Canderel and Nokia and through its registration list of 5,000 bloggers in about 10 countries it enlists participants to sample products in the hope they will be inspired to write about them. Blog placement is here to stay (IHT, 2006c).

- The Nokia Concept Lounge took place in the summer of 2005. Not surprisingly, in a GLOBAL BRAIN world, entries came from all over, with the winner being a Turkish designer, Tamér Nakisci. His wristband style phone (the 'Nokia 888') must have had phone manufacturers from China to Finland drooling. Remember, tomorrow's breakthrough designer, thanks to the spread and power of the internet, could just as easily come from equatorial Africa as from California.

- What goes for phones also goes for coffee. Nespresso's 2005 Design Contest, aimed at imagining the future of coffee rituals, yielded gems like the Nespresso InCar coffee machine and the Nespresso Chipcard (which stores coffee preferences for registered individuals, and when inserted into a vending machine, communicates with a central database to brew a personalized cup of coffee).

- Dutch supermarket chain Albert Heijn did something clever and sensible at the end of 2006: instead of installing suggestion boxes that customers don't use and stores don't empty, they asked customers for detailed feedback on how to improve their stores, through websites, leaflets and billboards. More than 55,000 customers took the bait, commenting on service, assortment and convenience levels in over 700 stores in the Netherlands. Seven hundred submitters of 'Golden Tips' (which are online for all to see) won one-minute shopping sprees, with individual stores committing to implement suggestions as soon as possible.

- The Electrolux Design Lab 2005 attracted entries from over 3,058 design students from 88 countries around the world, the top six countries being the United States, the UK, China, India, Brazil and Italy. Participants were asked to design household appliances for the year 2020. Twelve finalists participated in a six-day design event in Stockholm, including workshops, model building and a competition for cash awards, appliances and more.

- A few companies have truly integrated this way of thinking into everything they do. One of the leaders in integrating CUSTOMER-MADE into its corporate fabric, P&G, is not slowing down: its Connect + Develop programme and other innovation projects now produce more than 35 per cent of the company's innovations. In fact, R&D productivity at Procter & Gamble has increased by nearly 60 per cent. In the past two years, P&G launched more than 100 new products for which some aspect of development came from outside the company. Among P&G's most successful connect-and-develop products to hit the market are Olay Regenerist, Swiffer Dusters, the Crest SpinBrush and the Mr. Clean Magic Eraser (source: *HBR*, March 2006).

- P&G also recently rebranded its Tremor Moms programme to Vocalpoint. In their own words: 'Vocalpoint is a unique marketing brand powered by the Procter & Gamble Company that helps companies do a better job developing products and services that moms care about and want to talk about. We work with this influential group of moms to help companies in industries that include entertainment, fashion, music, food and beauty. We collect feedback and generate valuable knowledge and insight for our clients through surveys, product sampling and previews of products and services.' P&G is the champion of CUSTOMER-MADE, to the point of selling its co-creation expertise to others. Not bad.

- Philips-owned LeadUsers.nl has just completed its second lead-user-centric project, which was all about discussing the quality of sleep. The site has been active since August 2005, and aims to bring together lead users (those consumers that face the needs that will be general in the marketplace, but face them months or years ahead of the rest of the marketplace, and are positioned to benefit significantly by obtaining a solution to those needs) to discuss various topics of interest to both Philips and participants. The first topic of discussion and research was video telephony: a number of participants received the latest in video telephony equipment to be tested at home. The website will give you some good cues for setting up your own lead users' community, so sign up!

- Another example of create and sell: LEGO's LEGO Factory has been around for a while, but it remains an inspiring example of how to truly unleash THE GLOBAL BRAIN. Children and other building enthusiasts visiting the site are invited to design models (using easy-to-use, free downloadable software) and take part in competitions for LEGO prizes. A popular contest last year entitled winners to have their model mass produced and sold in Shop@Home, receiving a 5 per cent royalty on each set sold.

- Danish Vores Øl ('Our Beer') claims to be the world's first open-source beer. The recipe and the entire brand are published under a Creative Commons licence, meaning that anyone can use Vores Øl's recipe to brew the beer or to create a derivative. As long as home brewers publish the recipe under the same licence, they're free to make money from their efforts, which includes free access to Vores Øl's design and branding elements. Cheers!

- In the UK, Orange has set up Talking Point, where customers can tell Orange how they feel about all sorts of things – not just phones. Orange promises to listen, and to use the info to shape the way they think about and do things in the future. A number of questions (like 'what in your life would you like to see technology improve?') make it easier for visitors to share their thoughts. This isn't really a sparkling conversation, but it's better than nothing, in what is still very much a one-way arena.

- From April to October 2005, Itaú, Brazil's largest bank, launched a campaign titled 'O Itaú quer ouvir você', which means (how refreshing!) 'Itaú wants to listen to you'. Through a massive ad campaign, and by using channels such as dedicated 0800 numbers, e-mail and online chats, employees at their banks and actual telephones at ATMs, Itaú went far beyond the usual concept of suggestion boxes. They even promised to get back to participants in five working days, commenting on suggestions made. First results: an average of 7,200 requests, complaints and suggestions per month.

- IKEA's 'fiffigafolket' contest (Swedish for 'ingenious people'), which has just come to an end and is now in jury-phase, asked amateur outsiders to send in clever designs for storing home media (hi-fi sets, TV, DVDs etc) in the living room. Out of 5,000 ideas submitted, 14 winners will be invited to IKEA headquarters for a workshop, and will receive €2,500. More interestingly, the designs will actually get produced and end up in IKEA stores for all to see, buy and assemble. (Source: Springspotter Network, Okee Williams.)

- And even airplanes! Last year, 120,000 people around the world signed up to join Boeing's World Design Team, an internet-based global forum that encourages participation and feedback while the company is developing its new airplane. Activities include message boards, conversations with the Boeing design team, and extensive discussions on what members like and don't like about air travel today, as well as features they'd like to see in their dream airplane. In Boeing's own words: 'Flyers and aviation enthusiasts from around the world are sharing the excitement of creating the aeroplane of the future.'

And so on and so on. This type of genuine interaction with your shopper is here to stay. Introduce your shopper-made programme now. Go out there and co-create with your shoppers now. CO-CREATE SHOPPER-MADE.

5 REevaluating the shopping experience

> I would rather be vaguely right than precisely wrong.
>
> John Maynard Keynes

- Today, brands are squeezed by retailers, private labels, media and shoppers.
- Brands need to reconnect to their shoppers.
- Brands need to move from a focus on brand awareness to a focus on brand selection.
- Successful brands in the future will be those with relevant new actionable shopper insights.
- Successful brands will be those that own the shopping experience.

Brands need to master the shopping experience and all the brand touch points – pre, during and post the experience (Figure 5.1). They also need, as we explained in *Retailization*, to reverse their thinking and start their understanding and strategic development at the post stage, where the true success of a brand really happens, ie the building of loyalty and repeat sales. That's why the arrows go anticlockwise. It's on the shelf where it all starts and ends. At the moment that experience is mastered to a large extent by the retailer, particularly in-store. To master that experience brands need to

brand success in the future belongs to those who
master the shopping experience

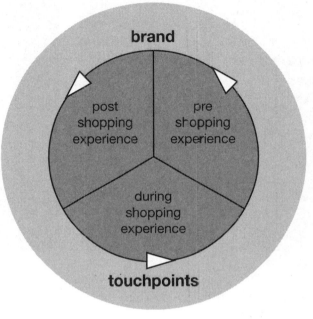

Figure 5.1   The shopping experience

know more – they need their own unique knowledge to counter the
retailers' scanning data. Brands need a new weapon – a knowledge weapon
that will allow them to forge an effective two-sided alliance of knowledge
with their key partners in selling.

That weapon is Brand Shoppability™, or to put it another way, 'HOW
MUCH DO SHOPPERS WANT TO SHOP FOR YOUR BRAND?'

When considering the shopping experience we have to view it as a three-
stage process, each step having key stimuli that influence the shopper
directly (Figure 5.2). We not only need to fully understand what exactly
those stimuli are, but also measure their effect. Retail historically has been
viewed primarily as a sales channel, with transaction data the standard
metric of evaluation. The shopper today is a very different person from
what he or she was a few decades ago, and measuring the importance of the
store as a marketing channel has taken on a new importance.

Consumers have changed in recent decades. As additional options have
become available, media usage patterns have changed dramatically. Thus,
the task of building and maintaining brand awareness among consumers
has become harder. As the pace of life quickens, consumers have less time to

brand shoppability™ during the shopping experience

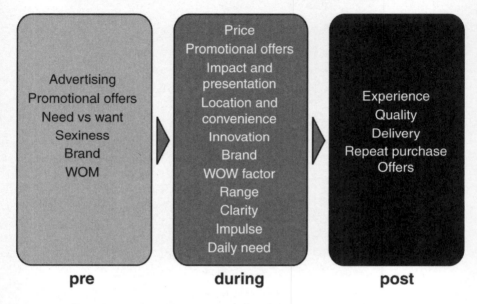

pre	during	post
Advertising Promotional offers Need vs want Sexiness Brand WOM	Price Promotional offers Impact and presentation Location and convenience Innovation Brand WOW factor Range Clarity Impulse Daily need	Experience Quality Delivery Repeat purchase Offers

Figure 5.2 Key stimuli throughout the shopping experience

devote to any single activity and are demanding that the information they receive from marketers be more relevant and personally beneficial.

These changes in consumer behaviour have led marketers and retailers increasingly to embrace the concept of the retail environment as a vehicle for building brand equity in addition to selling products. But this potential can't be fully evaluated without metrics that allow for comparison with other media options. It starts, however, with fully understanding the shopping experience itself.

While the store is one of the oldest marketing environments, it is the least understood from an effectiveness standpoint. Since consumers spend time in stores, it is important to understand how better to provide what they need, when they need it and in the form that best meets those needs. As retailers already know, **knowledge is power**. Those who know are able to control, or, at the very least, influence. At the moment, brands have very little influence when it comes to the shopping experience. They frankly haven't really known what's happening in store. They assumed it was out of their control and in the control of retailers and their research suppliers (ie Nielsen).

That is about to change!

PRISM

The first of these changes is a unique attempt in the United States to measure the audience for in-store marketing (In-Store Metrics Consortium, 2006). A consortium of manufacturers and retailers spear-headed by the In-Store Marketing Institute has created a tool for measuring in-store consumer reach at the category level. The model was verified by research conducted at four leading retailers in the spring of 2006. Officially christened as Pioneering Research for an In-Store Metric (PRISM), the measurement model is the brainchild of the In-Store Metrics Consortium, an ad hoc coalition formed under the Institute's guidance involving retailers Albertsons, Kroger, Walgreens and Wal-Mart and manufacturers 3M, Walt Disney, Coca-Cola, Kellogg, Miller Brewing and P&G.

The new measurement model predicts consumer reach by category or area of the store, by retail format, and by day of the week, delivering an unprecedented unique insight into the store as a marketing channel. The model could prove to be a watershed event for the marketing world, because it allows the store to be compared alongside television, radio and other forms of mass media for its ability to deliver consumer reach. In effect, it could do for the store what the measurement of gross ratings points (GRP) did for television.

While in-store marketing has long been an element of the consumer marketing mix, its potential value as a brand-building vehicle has never been objectively assessed, largely because there hasn't been a way to measure accurately the total reach of a campaign conducted at retail. By establishing a common metric that can be understood by both brand marketers and retailers, this model might eliminate that obstacle.

> This project will unleash new potential for retailers and marketers to create a simpler, more enjoyable shopping experience for people. It will give marketers a better understanding of the in-store environment that is certain to have a meaningful impact on the consumer. I applaud the industry collaboration that it took to make this new measurement initiative possible.
>
> Jim Stengel, global marketing officer for Procter & Gamble

Was it collaboration or desperation?

In spring 2006 the consortium's research team began working on the theory that by predicting in-store traffic and then determining what marketing communications are in the store – ie measuring compliance – a calculation could be made on the 'opportunities to see' a specific communication. By using existing statistical models that factor out duplicate impressions (accounting for multiple 'visits' to the area by the same people), a 'gross ratings point', or GRP, could be calculated for specific locations in the store. GRPs are the standard measurement used in the TV industry to assess the potential reach of advertising. The initial hypothesis was that reliable traffic estimates could be achieved by using data already collected through point-of-sale (POS) systems and other easily obtainable information, such as store format, product category, units sold and number of category baskets.

This hypothesis was validated through a pilot study that counted traffic in 63 product categories in 10 stores using infrared sensors positioned in aisles, perimeter locations and store entrance and exit zones. Adoption of the PRISM model by the industry would deliver a common language for retailers, manufacturers and media buyers to assess the value of retail as a marketing channel and compare its effectiveness to other media such as TV, radio and print. It also would give marketers a metric through which to evaluate the store as a vehicle for generating brand awareness and trial, putting the store on a level playing field with other forms of mass media.

'As the consumer increasingly demands more from marketing messages, and assumes more control over how she chooses to receive them, it's clear that we need to not only understand but master the effectiveness of engagement touch points. In-store marketing is a critical communications device and deserves a seat at the table,' said Laura Desmond, CEO of media planning agency Starcom/Mediavest USA. 'Through this research, based on carefully tested methodology and rich with insights, we now have a powerful metric to build smarter, consumer-centric in-store programs for our clients.'

For example, a snack foods brand might find that it can reach the same number of consumers over a one-week period by running a certain number of 30-second spots on broadcast TV, print ads in 20 magazines, or aisle displays in three leading supermarket chains. Based on the campaign's objectives, budgetary guidelines and return-on-investment goals, the brand could then determine which media options make the most sense. By analysing audience reach in concert with sales data, marketers will be able to identify the relative effectiveness of various in-store communications. The consortium is confident that it can be applied to all traditional retail channels. A deep understanding of traffic levels in stores will allow product manufacturers to assess the value of in-store marketing more effectively, including its value as a vehicle for building brand awareness and trial. It also gives manufacturers and retailers a common language with which to assess marketing opportunities and work together to better meet shopper needs. Members of the consortium believe that the ability to measure the in-store audience could be a marketing milestone as significant as the rise of television as an advertising vehicle in the 1950s. The consortium hopes to begin the next study early in 2007.

'This study has tremendous importance for retailers. Informed by the sophisticated data that this new metric will provide, retailers, for the very first time, now can consider new store layouts and product adjacencies to create an in-store experience that is more relevant, and thus, even more satisfying,' said Stephen Quinn, senior vice president of marketing for Wal-Mart. 'Our organization has scrutinized the methodology of this study. We find its implications for both retailers and consumers are far-reaching. We are eager to move forward with the next phase that will refine and expand the application of the metric.'

On the other side of the world in Sweden they are developing their own unique approach to help brands deal with extreme retailer concentration. They call that approach the BSI™.

Brand Shoppability Index™

The Brand Shoppability Index has been developed by DLF, the Grocery Manufacturers of Sweden, with direct cooperation between Keith Lincoln and Movement.nu, a leading Scandinavian shopper research agency. This group set out to ask a very basic question about shoppability.

'HOW MUCH DO SHOPPERS WANT TO SHOP FOR YOUR BRAND?'

In order to answer this question they developed the Brand Shoppability Index™ or BSI – a quantifiable actionable measure of a brand's shopping experience. In essence, a quantified and verified measure of the key factors that determine the effectiveness of a brand's shopping experience, PRE, DURING AND POST THE EXPERIENCE.

The BSI will identify key shopper action stimuli at each step of the shopping experience and, where possible, quantify the key stimuli in the shopping decision process today and tomorrow. They will then use that quantification to establish a brand shoppability index to measure the effectiveness of the shopping experience, which will provide a measure that leads to actionable responses. Several key areas were examined to try to understand what really influences the shopping experience, from the nature of choice to shopping environment evolution to shopper psychology evolution to evaluating shopper needs vs wants to the role of retailer brands and the role of impulse.

The BSI has been designed to directly measure the shopping experience and to provide brand suppliers with actionable, cost-effective, relevant and updated attitude and behaviour shopper insights by retailer chain and store format and optionally by categories and brands (Figure 5.3). This study will be completed during 2007 and is backed by the leading food companies in Sweden.

All BSI™-category perspective

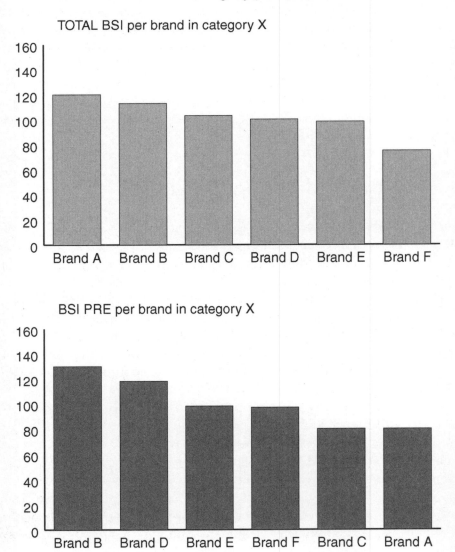

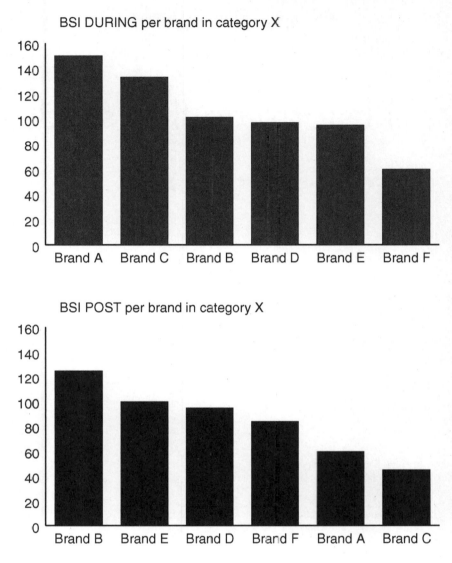

Figure 5.3 Hypothetical output from BSI

Clearly a lot is happening out there and there's a lot more to come as brands try to gain their power back, particularly their knowledge power. Do you want to be shoppable? Make brand shoppability your call to action.

6 REstorming the trends

We can't come up with good retail ideas until we truly understand the trends. Trends that lead to actionable, RElevant insights. Simply... Tip, Blink and Luck.

> The future ain't what it used to be.
>
> Yogi Bera (1925)
>
> The future belongs to those who dare.
>
> Anonymous
>
> The future belongs to those who prepare for it today.
>
> Malcolm X

We can talk all the retail actions in the world, but they're pretty useless unless they're on the right track. That track is the track of being sure your direction reflects the global trends that matter. The global trends that actually make a difference. The trends that have real RElevance to your future.

We recently helped develop a proprietary tool to help produce those actionable, relevant insights we believe we need to help us create better shopping and retail experiences for brands. This was developed in conjunction with Opinion Bengal, one of Scandinavia's leading trend companies. It works on the basis that three areas of understanding are critical if we want to produce breakthrough areas of future development.

It is according to the shapes that I lay plans for victory, but the multitude does not comprehend this.

Sun Tzu

Those three areas are:

1. understanding the long-term trends;
2. understanding the consumer and category you operate in;
3. understanding retail and shopping trends.

Once you truly understand those three areas you can apply that knowledge through a process called TIP, BLINK & LUCK™ to derive and drive future actionable marketing and retail initiatives (Figure 6.1).

Tip is a part of the process that borrows thinking from Malcolm Gladwell's book *The Tipping Point*, where he argues how important it is to understand and identify the key tipping points that lead to trends. Not all bits of 'odd behaviour' signal an emerging trend. There are certain principles, conditions and factors that mean some of the small emerging trends become full-scale social trends.

Opinion Bengal calls these Trend Creation Principles:

Principle #1. Reflecting unmet needs. Does the emerging trend capture an unmet need or help solve a problem?

Principle #2. Going with the flow. Does the emerging trend mesh with the dominant social values and themes of the era?

Principle #3. Transmission personnel must be in place. Are the 'right' people in place to transmit the ideas and behaviours to the rest of society?

Principle #4. Assistance of the media. Will the media (especially the entertainment media) be active in spreading the idea, lifestyle and behaviour?

Principle #5. Does it resonate on many levels? Does the emerging trend work on multiple levels? Intellectual ('It makes sense'), Emotional ('It feels right') and Practical ('It fits into my life – solves problems').

Blink refers to Malcolm Gladwell's second book *Blink* (2006), where he explains why bringing the right level of experience to provide the intuition is critical to really understanding things. This is particularly the case in

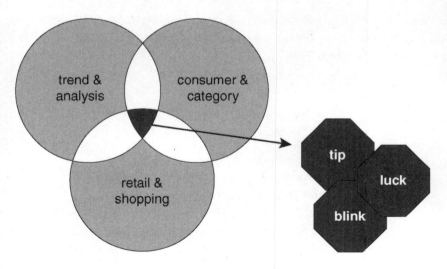

Figure 6.1   Trends that lead to actionable insights

retail matters, where experience really counts. Knowing what works is an intuitive process to a certain extent, gleaned from direct operational experience. Real experience also shows us whether the trend is truly relevant or not. We can spend a lot of time chasing wild ideas… but isn't it better that we chase wild ideas that might work?

Using intuition and experience means paying attention to your feelings and knowing their accuracy, and how well to apply them. An important assumption when using intuition is that you already know the answer. George Washington solved his most difficult problems during the Revolutionary War of Independence with intuition. He would instruct his orderlies not to let anyone disturb him while he relaxed and intuited decisions. In fact, the founding fathers thought intuition was so important that they sought to remind us on the back of a US dollar bill. There is a picture of an unfinished pyramid with an eye above it. The pyramid is not complete until the seeing eye is settled in the capstone position. Or, until the intuitive component of the mind plays a major role in developing ideas or making decisions.

Isenberg identified five different ways that successful managers use intuition:

- to help them sense when a problem exists;
- to rapidly perform well-learnt behaviour patterns;
- to synthesize isolated bits of data and experience into an integrated picture;
- to check on the results of rational analysis;
- to bypass in-depth analysis and come up with a quick solution.

Charles Merrill of Merrill Lynch once said that if he made decisions fast, he was right 60 per cent of the time. If he took his time, analysed the situation and made a decision carefully, he would be right 70 per cent of the time. However, the extra 10 per cent was seldom worth the time.

Finally, the third part of the process – **luck** – refers to the fact that we believe that you can optimize your true luck by having all the factors working for you optimally. In essence, what does it take to produce a retail phenomenon that works? Brands that have succeeded have always had luck on their side, sometimes by default and sometimes by design. Yes, luck is chance... but it's also about giving yourself the best chance. Any professional gambler will tell you that.

Arguably there are nine things that are truly important:

- Be the trend leader.
- Be different.
- Have a strategy.
- Understand your customer.
- Be streetwise.
- Time it right.
- Powerful communications.
- Creative electricity.
- Have courage.

These factors emerge from looking at literally hundreds of phenomenal brands going back as far as the 60s and including Nike, Disney and the Beatles, for example. Get all these things right and you'll end up with a truly great retail strategy, many more times than you'll end up with a bad one (Figure 6.2).

The food industry at the moment is a good example of an industry wide open to the influence of trends on its retail strategies. Paul Lincoln, CEO of the National Heart Forum in England, recently summarized the trends for the future as he saw them:

1. Junk food will become the new tobacco and there will be increased media and political interest in the junk food culture. There will be vastly increased monitoring and exposure of industry commitments and actions on products and brands.
2. Ever-tightening statutory regulation on marketing, health claims, labelling in Europe and the increased prospect of litigation in the United States. The prospect of a global food and health treaty in the wake of the ever-increasing worldwide chronic disease epidemics.

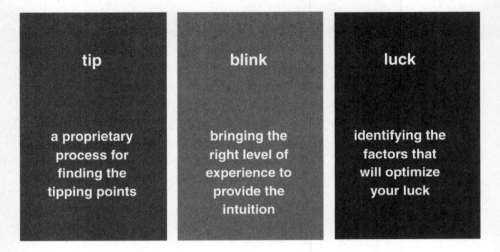

Figure 6.2   The tip, blink and luck process

Health-care costs will continue to soar and governments will want to take action owing to the large extrinsic social costs of this type of food production and the damaging macroeconomic implications for their economies.

3. The food industry will more visibly divide into junk (health-damaging) food producers and health-promoting food producers. Possibly the same for retailers? The companies will need to be clear about their future core business, market themselves accordingly and redefine their brand values. The social reform agenda is set. The critical issue is how the junk-food-orientated companies perceive the risk if they are going to adapt to or fight change or stick with their core business. There will be much greater investment in R&D and product reformulation as consumer demand will increase owing to higher health literacy.

Believe me, these trends are relevant to any food company's future. With trends like this, you'd better make the right decisions! And take action.

So TIP your brands in the right retail direction, make your BLINK intuition and experience work for you, and optimize your LUCK.

Be RElevant for tomorrow's actions.

7 REcreating the brand message

This is one area where retailers can learn from brands, and brands can use what they were always good at to make them better brands at the retail level.

> Don't worry about people stealing an idea. If it's original, you will have to ram it down their throats.
>
> Howard Aiken (1900–73)

We sometimes forget that it's brands that invented positioning, brand strategies, single-minded propositions and all that. Some retailers have been good at taking those philosophies and bringing them alive for themselves. Those ideas can be described as retail ideas that are bigger than advertising, from Sony PlayStation with 'Powerful Experiences' to Tesco with 'Making Shopping Easier' to Apple with 'Total Involvement' to P&G with 'The Moments of Truth'. We call those ideas the BRI™ – BIG RETAIL IDEAS.

The big retail idea

We should think of our businesses as businesses that create big retail ideas that sell things for our clients. Big retail ideas are platforms for the total development of brands and businesses beyond how they advertise them- selves. That's because genuinely big retail ideas drive more than adver- tising and communications. At their best, big retail ideas tell you more than what to say as a brand – they tell you how to behave as a business. At their very best, big retail ideas can become the prime driving force for your organizations.

No mere mortal has backed this thought. As Jack and Suzy Welch said recently (*Daily Telegraph*, 2006a), it's that killer idea – a 'big aha' as we call it – that gives you a sustainable competitive advantage. Put another way: strategy is just a winning value proposition, that is, a product or service that customers simply want more than any other options out there. Beyond that, strategy is all in its execution. And we all know where the field of execution is: RETAIL.

But, ideas don't grow on trees... REstorm

We have moved from mass production and mass marketing to mass participation. To succeed in this era, organizations need to embrace innovation and creativity. Nowhere is that more important than finding big retail ideas that drive your very ability to sell. We know that big retail ideas don't grow on trees, so we've developed a process that allows us to apply our two key principles to the finding of big retail ideas – first that a big idea doesn't mind who had it and secondly that the best way to get a big retail idea is to get a lot of ideas. It's called the BIG RETAIL IDEA™ (BRI) process and it's based on the theory that a big retail idea comes from research, thinking, experience and creativity in three areas that work together:

- understanding the brand as a retail brand;
- understanding the brand's shopper;
- understanding the brand's retail environment.

At the heart of our process lies the Big Retail Ideas Day – when you can work towards developing the big retail idea. In essence, we REstorm, or retail brandstorm, your retail future (Figure 7.1).

Ideas into action

There's little point coming up with big new retail ideas if you can't put them into action. So you must also think ahead and use partners to help this process. Frankly, there's too much action for one partner communications agency alone. If retail becomes the centre of your business, it becomes the centre of all your activities. You need the best partners you can find. Here in Sweden we have formed collaborative creative partnerships with some of

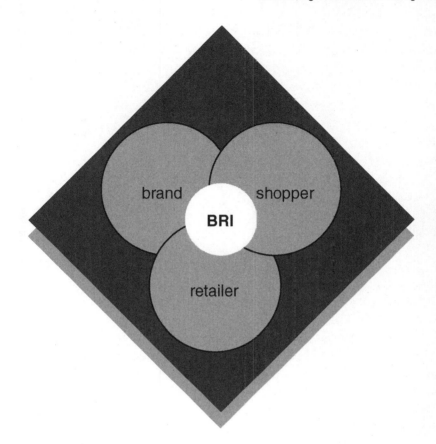

Figure 7.1   The BRI

Scandinavia's leading companies to help us turn ideas into actions. The first of these is Opinion Bengal, Scandinavia's leading trend company, which works with us and the client to identify the actionable insights that will drive the client's brand and retail development efforts. Once the ideas have been formulated and brainstormed (a process we call REstorming) via our Big Retail Ideas Day, we work closely with SWE, Sweden's leading communications agency, and Boden & Co, Sweden's leading events agency, to help the client realize the most creative and effective results from product development to communications to retail impact. If the client needs shopper research we use the best in Scandinavia – Movement.nu. We have focused all this through a small virtual agency called SWERETAIL, whose prime task is the development of the BRI (SWERETAIL.COM).

We develop the BRI by focusing on the key cornerstones, as we call them – the cornerstones that allow us to develop, analyse and measure retail thinking in practice (Figure 7.2).

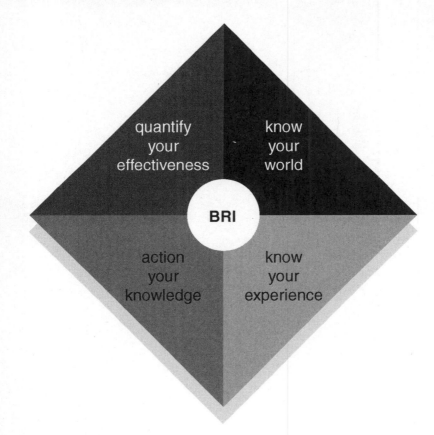

Figure 7.2   The BRI cornerstones

They are, in chronological order:

- Know your world.
- Know your experience.
- Action your knowledge.
- Quantify your effectiveness.

Each one is supported by a key process, all four of which we've already mentioned (Figure 7.3):

Tip, blink and luck TO HELP YOU KNOW YOUR WORLD
Shoppability   TO HELP KNOW YOUR EXPERIENCE
Retailization   TO HELP YOU ACTION YOUR KNOWLEDGE
BSI   TO HELP YOU QUANTIFY YOUR EFFECTIVENESS

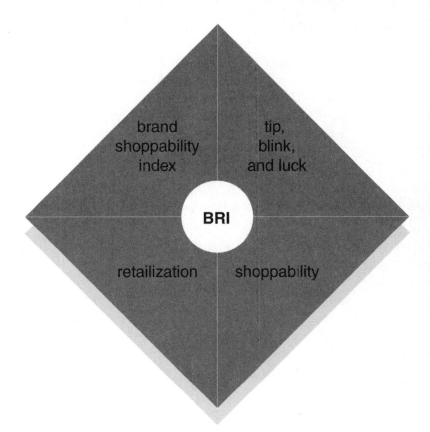

Figure 7.3 The BRI proprietary techniques

By applying our process we not only get nearer the idea, but we let creativity become the driving force. It should be. Too many retail ideas are driven by short-termism, tactics rather than strategy and design agencies' requirements.

REvisiting retailization

Let's pause for a few moments and revisit the subject of our first book – retailization. The retailization process is the critical action cornerstone. It allows us to focus on what exactly we need to do to win (Figure 7.4).

In that book, we defined seven key steps that will help you to achieve retailization: seven steps built on three different mindsets. You may believe you are already covering all seven steps and you most probably are. However, we believe our process adds a new rigour and creative and intellectual

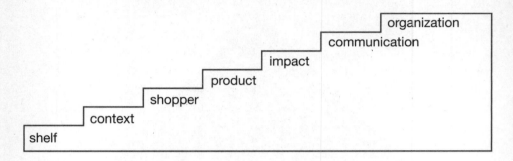

Figure 7.4   The seven-step retailization process

intensity to an issue that merits it. Retailization is not a pick-and-mix kind of process. You must thoroughly complete all the steps to reach your retail objectives and embrace retailization as the long-term guiding philosophy to take you along the pathway to better sale(s). Part 2 of this book looks directly at 25 case studies of brands and retailers who are excelling at retail and applying some of the principles we outline. Part 3 of this book will show you how to make the process work for you operationally. We believe that by following the process you can go a long way towards mastering the shopping experience (Figure 7.5).

- Are you ready to roll up your sleeves?
- Are you ready to redefine marketing?
- Are you ready to retailize?

Active retail thinking

In order to get original ideas, you need to be able to look at the same information everyone else does and organize it into a new and different pattern. That is active thinking.

A good football manager does not say 'there is one way to win and we must do the same'. He tries instead to determine which of his players are strong and which are weak by testing and observing each individual player. Then he replaces the weaker players or teaches them to overcome their weakness. Only in this way can the coach bring his team's unique talents into play. A football team has one goal: to win. It is the same with retail. You must be aware of the negative and positive forces operating in any retail challenge you face, before you develop a strategy for solving it. Your

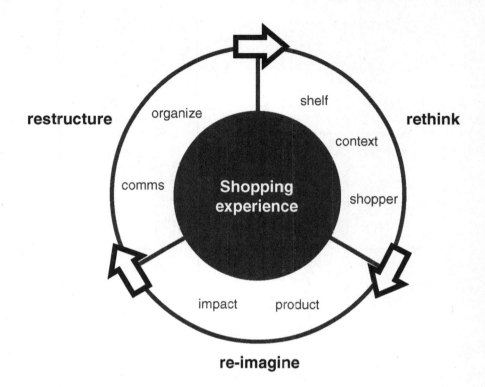

Figure 7.5 The retailization process

strategy should allow you to take advantage of the positive factors while eliminating the negative ones. It's a virtual tug of war!

The grid shown in Figure 7.6 helps you do just that:

1. to better define your challenges;
2. to identify strengths you can maximize;
3. to identify strengths you can minimize.

Try assembling a grid for your retail challenge, the challenge between you and your shoppers. Then build a grid for the challenge between your brand and the retailer's brand: your tug of war.

There are three ways to move towards the best-case scenario you should bear in mind. They are:

1. Maximize your strengths.
2. Minimize your weaknesses.
3. Add more positive forces.

TUG OF WAR			
Challenge: probability of getting a major sale			
winning the sale	+	−	losing the sale
superior	◄ product		inferior
none		competition ►	superior
lowest	◄ shopper need	price ►	highest
real	◄ shopper knowledge		little or none
high	◄ shopper budget		low
able to buy			not able to buy
excellent		sales presentation ►	poor
able to overcome	◄ answering objections		not able to overcome
liked by shopper		shopper compatibility ►	disliked by shopper

Figure 7.6   The retail tug-of-war grid
Source and inspiration: Thinkertoys

You can, of course, choose to strengthen your positive forces even more. Equally, you can minimize your weaknesses by reframing them as challenges:

- In what ways might I improve my customer relationships?
- In what ways might I improve my creativity?
- In what ways might our product be perceived as superior?
- In what ways might we add value to the product to further justify its price?
- In what ways can I involve shoppers?

Doing all three is the key, however. When Steve Wozniak and Steve Jobs created Apple Computers back in 1976, they had a principal strength – a unique design for a personal computer, and a major weakness – only $1,300 to invest. But they succeeded by maximizing their principal strength by selling 50 (unbuilt as yet) computers to a string of hobby stores based on their design, minimizing their weakness by securing credit to buy parts, based on sales of unbuilt computers, and finally adding a positive force by using the profits gained from the sale of the first 600 computers to start work on what became the very successful Apple 11.

Active retail thinking is the key.

From USP to RSP

> For a marketing strategy to have any hope of succeeding, retailers need a unique selling point – be it price, product range, location or service. Once that has been identified, it is up to the marketing department to do its job and demonstrate the effectiveness of its marketing spend.
>
> David Bush, head of retail research at the consultant Grant Thornton. (IHT, 2006c)

Brands have long been defined through their USPs or Unique Single-minded Propositions – a system developed by the advertising industry to help them focus their creatives on producing targeted meaningful executions. We need to revisit the whole notion of the USP aimed at consumers and evolve that thinking to fit with the new reality – shoppers and retail focus. This expression will not be the often boring bland USP documents that agencies use to brief creatives.

USP to RSP

- USP
  - consumer targeted;
  - consumer proposition;
  - desired consumer response;
  - consumer tone of voice;
  - media actions.
- RSP (Retail Selling Proposition)
  - shopper targeted;

- retail proposition;
- desired shopper response;
- tone of voice to shoppers;
- retail communications actions.

A briefing form would make all this clearer. The content of the RSP is based on our retailization journey and has seven discrete parts based on the seven steps, plus a BRI to sum it up. Each part has a short single sentence to describe what your brand has done to achieve this step.

The RSP briefing form

- Shelf: what new thinking have you developed? Are there new shelves you should be on?

- Context: what new thinking have you developed to better compete?

- Shopper: what new thinking/insights have you developed about your shopper?

- Product: what have you re-imagined and will it work in a retail environment?

- Retail: describe your revolutionary selling situation?

- Communications: what communications approaches do you recommend to excite your shoppers and drive them to your shelves?

- Organization: what changes and structures are you putting in place to optimize your organization's retail capabilities?

- BRI: a simple phrase that captures the essence of your big retail idea. It should be a vibrant, flexible, stimulating call to action.

We need RSPs aimed at shoppers, not consumers. These RSPs must be involving, entertaining and inspiring. We need to move to a more focused effort where your consumer USP is refocused towards being a unique selling proposition for the shopper: the RSP. The product as well as your communications is an important part of making the RSP work.

Apart from briefing communications agencies, the RSP will also help your designers understand retail better and help them understand it's not just a great product that's important – it's a great product that grabs the attention and interest of shoppers. They need to design for retail effectiveness from day one. They need to write retail objectives into their design briefs. They need a RSP.

The retail circle of opportunity

So where can your inspiration come from?

We have put eight key directions in our circle of opportunity (Figure 7.7). Simply spin it and see where it lands. Then think creatively in that direction. You might be surprised at what you come up with.

One word for all

Thinking about the BRI, we were very struck by a recent article by Maurice Saatchi. In his 40 years in advertising, Maurice Saatchi has been responsible for some of the industry's best-known slogans – phrases such as 'The world's favourite airline' and 'Labour isn't working'. Now, the executive director of M&C Saatchi is arguing that companies should boil down their brands to a single word (*Times*, 2006a).

He argues that things need to change. He states that the latest developments in neuroscience indicate that a teenager today, who has grown up in a multi-channel, digital environment, processes messages in a different way from his parents. His brain is physically different. It has rewired itself. It

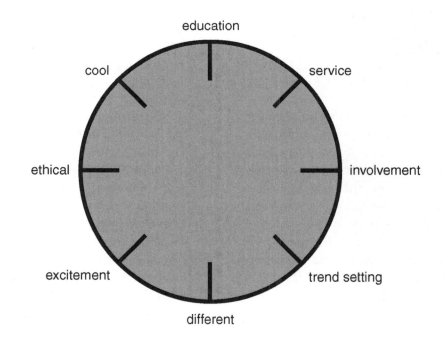

Figure 7.7   Retail circle of opportunity

responds faster. It sifts out. It recalls less. This is what makes it possible, apparently, for a modern teenager, in the 30 seconds of a normal TV commercial, to take a phone call, send a text, receive a photo, play a game, download a music track, read a magazine and watch commercials at 10× speed. They call it CPA (continuous partial attention).

The real challenge to the advertising industry is to find a way through. Saatchi's contention is that only the most brutally simple ideas stand a chance. In fact, he argues that the future of advertising, whatever the technology, will be to associate each brand with one word. He calls this one-word equity. One-word equity is the global ownership of one word in the consumer's mind.

It's the modern equivalent of having the best site on the high street, except that the location is in the mind and the consumer is the shopper.

There is more complexity now than ever before. And consumers can find out more easily than ever before about products and their performance. However, brands will remain a conspicuous feature of our age. Strong, simple brands will be a shortcut through the complexity and confusion in the marketplace.

> When a company owns one precise thought in the consumer's mind, it sets the context for everything and there should be no distinction between brand, product, service and experience. And finally, only the strongest companies will endure. The action of the market is Darwinian – the survival of the fittest.
>
> Maurice Saatchi

The strongest brands are defined by their ownership of one thought; the very strongest by one word. The nature of this thought or word predetermines the breadth of the brand's activities. This is why companies need to think very carefully about the dominant association they wish to create for their brand. If the word is attitudinal, it is possible it will have wider application. If it is product specific, it will define the company more tightly in its category.

With retailer consolidation and the growth of discounters and Private Label continuing in Europe, brands have to continue to hold market share. They can only do this by capturing people's imagination. This is only possible if it is clear what they stand for. The brands that achieve this will be higher profile, more talked about and more sought after. Only the simplest (a much-derided idea) will survive. Advertising must respect the intelligence of its audience, and if it does not prompt them to think, it will be instantly dismissed, particularly with the rise of the digital native, a new generation of consumers who multi-task and whose brains are programmed to edit ruthlessly. Only the simplest and most imaginative messages will get through and stand any chance of provoking thought – and the word of mouth that follows from it. This is particularly true when it comes to retail.

The one-word equity for the company acts as the brand's overarching strategic thought. All other facets of persuasion need to be reflected through this prism.

If the word does not have a clear meaning, universally understood in any language, it probably is not a very good word. This is exactly why companies have to think very carefully about the word they choose. And bear in mind, one-word equity does not mean a one-word slogan. The word may not even appear in the slogan. The important thing is that the brand's advertising prompts people to associate the precise meaning of the word with the brand. Saatchi has helped develop a process called WordWise. This involves applying brutal simplicity of thought to a company's proposition. It is the ruthless paring down from a paragraph to a sentence to a word. WordWise involves consumers and clients globally in this process.

It doesn't matter what the medium is that carries the message. The important thing is that one-word equity guides everything. Advertising at its best gives brands ruthlessly clear and simple positionings. And with the rise of the internet, one of a number of channels in a complex, fragmented marketplace, it will be even more important for brands to define themselves with ruthless clarity. The intellectual rigour of advertising – paring and editing down to a brutally simple thought – has never been more in demand. Of course, with the internet there are new and exciting forms of advertising – most notably interactive, but the underlying principles remain the same.

Advertising agencies have a schizophrenic attitude towards new media. This is because they fear message fragmentation. One-word equity solves this problem. It enables the marketing director to take full advantage of the new exciting channels while ensuring his or her brand retains single-minded clarity and message control.

Advertising agencies, using one-word equity, can then exploit these new channels with optimism and confidence. And they can particularly exploit them in the area of retail. Retail environments demand and beg for clear precise messages. How often do they get them? Not often enough, we fear. By RE-creating the brand message through an RSP and a BRI and then distilling that message into one-word equity, you can start to get to grips with your communications in a meaningful way, maybe for the first time. A brand like Apple really works because it has managed to ensure that its one-word equity is as apparent and relevant in its advertising as it is in its retail execution.

Think about your brand – what's your one-word equity? Is it good enough to win? Is it a word that works in your retail environments? We have spent a lot of time recently trying to find the one-word equity that brands stood for at retail. We could often find it at the image level, but had considerable problems finding it at the retail level. We suspect the reason for this is a loss of clarity when the brand message is translated down to operational reality. The detail of execution has clouded the original thinking. It shouldn't have. That one word is just as relevant here, if not more so. Make sure, when your brand is present at retail and when it communicates with your ultimate consumer – the shopper, that it really delivers on your promise.

So, have you been creative enough when it comes to your retail business? Constantly think of new angles and use creative techniques to get at the big idea that matters. REstorm, REstorm, REstorm. The BRI should always be on the agenda.

8 REflagging it

Literally everyone can and everyone should rethink their distribution options, starting with the creation of a flagship. A flagship to show you and the world what's truly possible.

The most visible expression of your brand is its presence on the shelf. We argued in our first book that everyone should consider trying their own proprietary distribution channels. And we did mean everyone! We'd like to take you through that further because we believe brands that want to demonstrate leadership should be building that leadership into a flagship.

The flagship store of the past

It started with the spectacular launch of the Niketown concept in New York, London and other key cities around the world in 1998. Despite scepticism (suggesting it was no more than a 3-D advertising hoarding that added little to the profitability to the brand as a retailer), they're still there! As David Dalziel (the head of one of London's leading design agencies – Dalziel POW) said to us, 'Although questionable as a retail operation it certainly works as a brand-building tool. Their commitment to quality has paid off and the robust nature of their fit-out has ensured it is still standing, but more than that, the commitment to maintaining a fresh communications strategy has ensured a relevance and longevity no one predicted.'

Since the Niketown innovation there has been an explosion in flagship store concepts:

Swatch
Virgin megacentres

Levi's
Puma
Adidas
etc.

Throughout their brief history some stores are simply bigger selling centres, some are genuine attempts to build the brand and educate the public and others are a muddling mix of both. The really successful ones are brand magnets that act as next-generation flagships which encourage repeat visits and have moved from passive display to active participation.

Some interesting examples

Esprit

On Regent Street, London, Esprit have re-launched a visual assault on the UK market after years of decline and created a massive store of some life and humour. Their look is eclectic, meaning it looks like every other retailer depending which part of the store you are in. The test of this flagship will be how fresh it can remain and how they can avoid the visual clutter from just becoming tiresome.

River Island

On Oxford Street, River Island have launched their largest city store to date at the former JJB site. River Island are retailers, operators in the extreme, and that has resulted in a store that delivers significant turnover from a difficult building. Retailer thinking has driven the concept to marry image and efficiency – a new kind of retail brand store, in contrast to the Nike model. The image of the store is flexible and reactive, with seasonal colour, texture and graphics playing a big part in creating the personality.

Nokia

Nokia unveiled a high-profile, high-concept flagship on Chicago's Michigan Avenue in October 2006. They are planning additional stores in Helsinki, New York, Hong Kong and Moscow. They also plan to open a total of 18 similarly designed flagships around the world.

'Just a few years ago, consumers looking to purchase a mobile phone had a limited selection of voice-only devices from which to choose', said Cliff Crosbie, director of global retail and trade marketing, Nokia.

'Today the choices have increased exponentially. The Nokia flagship store concept was developed to offer consumers unparalleled selection and guidance in this complex environment, and to do it in a way that transforms the process of acquiring a wireless device from a task into a pleasure. One important goal of the Nokia flagship store programme is to determine the most impactful methods of retailing our product line, and sharing those lessons across Nokia's retail and operator channels', Crosbie said.

They are 1,200 square feet in size and provide plenty of opportunities for customers to interact with the products. Shoppers can even send text messages that end up appearing on a series of plasma screens that are positioned within the store as well as at other Nokia stores around the globe.

The store also includes an 'experience' area where sales assistants demonstrate the features of the phones and educate customers. The aim is to educate customers rather than move product: there are no quotas or commissions, and all salespeople must complete a six-week course that focuses on technical knowledge rather than salesmanship. 'Our favourite thing to hear customers say is "I didn't know you could do that"', says Nokia.

Nokia intends to use the flagship stores as test labs, of sorts, analysing information on which attitudes and strategies are most effective. They hope to then communicate these findings to other Nokia stores and partnered service providers, so that elements of the flagship model will eventually have a home at smaller retailers. Nokia believes the stores will act as a retail laboratory that will benefit its global retail distribution network

Orange

In the UK the mobile operator Orange is experimenting with shop concepts that create a better customer experience. The 'not another phone shop' is a laid-back place where you can try out working phones and talk to salespeople who are both intelligent and patient – surprisingly rare.

As one employee explained, 'they're not paid on commission and are rewarded for positive feedback from customers, so that helps change the game significantly to the shopper's advantage'.

The welcoming space is decorated with photos taken with camera phones and the expected orange furniture. Phones are displayed in lucite cases, but can then be found in drawers beneath. Customers are encouraged to come back often – in the shop you can grab a coffee while your mobile is charged and cleaned or you can learn how to load music and read e-mail on your particular device.

One commentator said: 'I think it's a great idea for cellular stores to post camera phone photos. I know that many cellular operators are looking at ways to provide a better customer experience (and increase sales!) at their stores.'

Apple

And finally, probably the most famous flagship store yet. Their latest opening is on Fifth Avenue, New York. Other centres include Soho in New York, San Francisco, Los Angeles, Chicago, Tokyo and London. Apple produced near-hysteria on opening in New York, five-hour queues in Ginseng, Tokyo and 200 people camping overnight in London. The Apple flagships include a bottom-floor participation zone, continuous lecture theatres, genius bars, child centres and special-use education centres such as film. Apple stores act as design labs for smaller stores and as centres to promote non-Apple-branded accessories. They are obsessed with their locations and they have to be the best or else it won't open; for example, after years of searching for a site in Paris they still haven't found the 'right' one.

So what is the future of flagship stores as we near their 10th anniversary (although IKEA might argue that they invented the concept some 40 years before!)?

Guidelines for future REflagging

Image plus money

Flagship stores are still being built, but increasingly they are judged not only by the impact they have on the brand profile but also by the contribution they can make to the profitability of the brand in retail. Brand building and financial viability are not mutually exclusive anymore. The flagship concept has been hijacked by the retailer with brand aspirations to create retail flagships, quite different in culture from a brand flagship.

Marketing investment

It is critical that a flagship store isn't seen as a capital investment alone – it is more important to see it as a marketing investment. Your values and mission are realized here and it should act a laboratory test for the future – a vehicle that will benefit your whole distribution network.

Strategy first

The appetite for new and improved retail environments is still strong and retail design continues to challenge advertising as the most direct route to a consumer's mind. It is here that the brand can really make connections.

However, it is important that design doesn't dictate strategy. Strategy comes first and you should make sure you get this right first and don't use the store as a way of developing the strategy... a rather expensive process! Use our strategy grid, derived from the FCB (foot cone belding) positioning grid, to position your delivery and image today and your desired delivery and image tomorrow. We recommend the top right quadrant (Figure 8.1).

PDS it...

Do a problem detection study (PDS) to help you fully understand the problems today's shoppers face. Your real opportunity is solving the shoppers' problems. Your opportunity is not selling them an opportunity they don't really want. See the ASSA ABLOY case in Part 2 for more details.

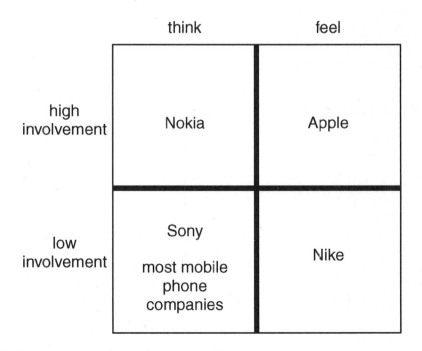

Figure 8.1 Retail involvement grid

Selling products not solutions

Too many flagship operators seem to focus their attention on creating interesting environments and fixture systems on which to place their products. The products are presented to shoppers the same way they are in any other store, just on design-y fixtures. Products are often not presented in the context of use; they are not bundled together with other products to create solutions; they are not presented in a way that helps consumers to understand what value they bring to their lives.

Remember you are appealing to shoppers

Products are often not presented in the context of use; they are not bundled together with other products to create solutions; they are not presented in a way that helps consumers to understand what value they bring to their lives and to visualize owning the products. Your reaction is usually, 'this is neat, but they really haven't done anything to help me in my shopping process'.

Learn from those who do it right

Some (but relatively few) brands do something other than present products. Apple, who offers the Genius Bar and Training Sessions, and The Whirlpool Insperience Studio, where you can wash clothes, cook dinner and otherwise use and interact with their products, are just two examples.

Keep the experience moving

A good flagship store should be changing/refreshing the experience; it should be an event/an experience. Most give you no reason to return, because you know you will have the same experience every time you come... maybe just a few different products.

Make the intangible tangible

The key to building a flagship is to make intangible values tangible and thereby easier to sell or buy. Develop based on need, location and goals.

Have a real mission

The Apple Center Program was created to identify and promote Apple resellers who deliver on the promise of the Apple brand. Apple Centers are expected to provide an exceptional buying experience for both new and existing Apple customers. Make sure you really understand everything first. Apple do! Here are some guidelines for a real mission:

1. Knowing your customers inside out: identifying market opportunities and target customers.
2. Powerful value proposition: your business statement to the market.
3. Balanced selection of products and services: focusing on profitable sources of revenue.
4. Knowledgeable and motivated people: building a winning team.
5. Smart and intuitive store design: creating an enjoyable store environment.
6. Eye-catching product attractions: selling through merchandising.
7. Compelling store experience: putting customers at ease.
8. Beyond the store: developing outbound sales activities.
9. Delivering on post-sales expectations: building a satisfied customer experience.
10. Constant obsession for detail: honouring the promise of the brand.

Well, are you up to it? Can you REflag your future and create your brand in reality?

9 REtrying again and again

Retailization spent a lot of time talking about the merging of buying and trying as a dynamic way to promote the brand and incite purchase. This is becoming an increasingly critical factor for sustainable success.

> There are only two moments of truth – buying and trying.
>
> A G Lafley, CEO, P&G

How to succeed in retail by really trying

When Tesco entices you through its doors for the bottle of Chardonnay advertised on the internet at €6, it is likely you will leave with more than you bargained for: a discounted Dyson vacuum cleaner perhaps, or a two-for-one deal on Indian meals (IHT, 2006b).

Retailers are clever at luring consumers. For superstores like Tesco, the British-based chain that is spreading rapidly throughout the world, the strength of its sales message can help it stand out in a saturated market and lift profit, despite tight margins and heightened competition for customers. Retailers who know their customers – and use that knowledge to craft marketing strategies – are finding greater sales and profits. But moving from being a success today to a great investment for tomorrow is a longer road, one paved with uncontrollables like rising operating costs, increased competition, market sentiment and fickle consumers.

After two years of falling sales, many analysts had given up hope on Marks & Spencer, the British food and fashion retailer. But the store has defied expectations with its latest advertising campaign featuring the 1960s fashion model Twiggy. Profit has soared since the store raised its advertising budget 30 per cent in 2005 to £45 million, or $78 million, and asked its suppliers to increase their discounts to 10 per cent from 5 per cent. The full jury decision remains out, though.

> M&S might not have dispelled all concerns about its future growth, but for investors at least, the company has made a decent fist of showing that it is back on track.
> Simon Irwin, a retail analyst at J.P. Morgan in London.

Wal-Mart Stores is another retailing giant that has seen better days, but, like M&S, it is not about to retire from the fight. Once a proponent of the 'pile 'em high, sell 'em cheap' philosophy, Wal-Mart has decided to go upmarket to compete with Target and Kmart, both of which have enlisted name designers to spruce up their low-price offerings. In addition to a glitzy advertising campaign in luxury publications like *Vogue*, Wal-Mart has focused on improving the quality of its merchandise and presenting smaller sizes and brighter colours.

The use of celebrities in advertisements may make Wal-Mart share-holders shudder – last year the advertising budget was $1.4 billion, compared with $888 million at Target – but some others argue that the change might give the retailer an edge.

> Wal-Mart is effectively redefining its future, and not before time.
> Howard Davidowitz, chairman of Davidowitz & Associates,
> a retail consultancy and investment bank in New York

Presentation of merchandise is one element of a successful retail strategy; harvesting customer information is another. Bryan Roberts, head of research at Planet Retail, a retail consultancy based in London, said Tesco Clubcard was a classic example of how marketing could feed an organization's strength. 'The loyalty card is used to drill down into Tesco's customer base and work out the purchase patterns of every male and female shopper from Aberdeen to Cornwall', he said. 'The data is then used for targeted promotional purposes.'

It might seem highly unlikely, but Tesco discovered that the purchase of diapers frequently coincided with the purchase of beer. 'Most of the purchases had been made by young men at around 6 in the evening,' Roberts said. 'The most likely scenario is that the men had been asked to pick up diapers on the way home from work.' Tesco sent discount vouchers for beer to the loyalty card holders. The supermarket also observed that shoppers who bought wild birdseed also bought organic foods, so discount vouchers for birdseed were sent to them. Would that a mere brand should have such information available to it.

Mining and refining the data is critical for a programme that can eat up a huge portion of a retailer's marketing budget. Simon Proctor, a retail analyst at Charles Stanley in London, said J Sainsbury, a competitor of Tesco, had been 'nowhere near as successful' with its loyalty card programme, which absorbs more than 50 per cent of the superstore's marketing expenditures.

The counter-argument to loyalty cards is that the money spent on managing programmes would be better directed towards cutting prices. Proctor is unconvinced. 'Low pricing is only successful up to a point', he said. 'Retailers also need promotions to stimulate interest.'

Bloom, a chain of grocery stores in North Carolina, has 'torn up the rule book as far as in-store design is concerned', Roberts said. 'When customers walk into the store, the first thing they are confronted with is a large circular table top stacked with convenience foods and wine. It has been a huge hit with customers and significantly enhanced Bloom's image.' The stores also reduced shelf heights, recognizing that most of their shoppers are female. And instead of dividing products by category, the stores use themes – for example, an aisle of breakfast items.

Selfridges in the UK have a similar approach with their innovative food sections. No boring old supermarket shelves here. Here they lay categories out in creative ways on long white fixtures, which look Swedish in design terms. For example, when it comes to olive oil, they let you choose the type you want or the blend you want to make up, let you select the bottle you want and then package it for you... albeit at a much greater price than the supermarket round the corner. At least you feel you have selected something for you that was very special. RE-me again!

Many retailers appeal to the customer's emotions. Take Media Markt, the electronics division of the German retailing giant Metro. 'The store is not any less expensive than other stores of its kind, but it has a great gimmick which appeals to the German psyche,' said Ralf Stroneyer, an equities analyst at DIT Allianz Dresdner in Frankfurt. Research has shown that Germans have a greater dislike of paying taxes than do other nationalities, he said. The store's 16 per cent discount is the equivalent of not charging value-added tax, and its slogan – 'Germans do not pay VAT' – is 'infinitely more powerful' than the discount, Stroneyer said.

And then there is the internet, which retailers have been particularly creative at using – from online catalogues to e-mail alerts on specials.

The internet is the main marketing channel in the Nordic countries, where the retailing industry is not as well developed as elsewhere in Europe, according to Jonathan Reynolds, a lecturer at Said Business School at Oxford University. And potentially, as internet growth shows, it is taking over as a communications and selling medium. The latest information on internet advertising in the UK, for example, is expected to reach 14 per cent of all advertising expenditure this year and 25 per cent by 2010, well ahead of TV at 20 per cent. This is the highest level in the world today, and more than double that of the United States (IHT, 2006e) (Figure 9.1). About 3.9 per cent of visits to British online sites yield purchases, compared to 2.5 per cent in the United States, according to Coremetrics, an e-commerce tracking service. And with broadband connectivity at nearly 48 per cent of homes, compared with the United States at 44 per cent of homes, slowing down doesn't seem to be an option.

The US department store J.C. Penney is using its online business to attract younger customers, many of whom still see the store as a place where their mothers and grandmothers shopped. In early March 2006 the company set up a 15,000-square-foot, or 1,400-square-metre, 'virtual store' in Times Square in New York as part of its spring advertising campaign. The three-level temporary showroom allowed shoppers to buy merchandise at 22 interactive kiosks.

Here are a few more ideas from the world of Springwise.

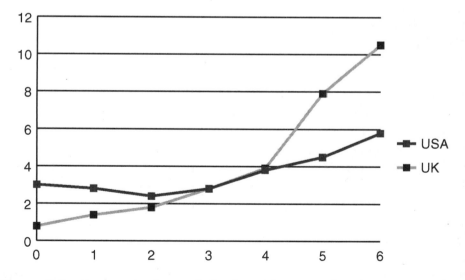

Figure 9.1 Internet's share of all advertising spending (per cent against years from 2000 onwards)

Sony launched its new range of DVD handy-cams by teaming up with London Zoo for 11 days in June 2005 to offer consumers the chance to borrow DVD handy-cams for one hour, free of charge. After a two-minute demonstration, families were free to roam the zoo and record all their favourite family moments. After their visit, the DVD handy-cam obviously had to be returned, but participants could keep their DVD (with pre-recorded product and purchase details). Says Sony: 'We had an amazingly successful time at the zoo. Around 95 per cent of visitors who trialled the DVD handy-cam said that they had never seen or heard of any promotional activity quite like this; they were astonished that we were actually going to lend them a handy-cam totally free of charge.'

Meanwhile, for more than two years, Canon has been inviting anyone in the EU to upload a digital picture to their website, pick a Canon printer they would like to try out, and fill in their address; a real photo print will then arrive in the mail the following day. Canon-owned online photo service Fotango fulfils and delivers. Owing to its ongoing success, the service has recently been expanded, increasing the range of Canon printers on trial. Seeing IS believing.

Maytag, the American appliance manufacturer, is beckoning consumers to literally test-drive products before making a choice. Try-out stores, owned by independent dealers, display Maytag merchandise in 'vignettes' of home kitchens and laundry rooms. Potential buyers of washers and dryers can do a load of laundry, bake a sheet of cookies, or listen to a dishwasher in action to see whether it really is quiet. The stores are about the size of a department-store appliance section (on average 6,000 square feet), but the atmosphere is more like a mom-and-pop shop. Maytag says the 'try-before-you-buy' concept is helping to close sales, and plans call for 60 Maytag stores, and another 30 to 40 locations next year. (Source: *Denver Post, Appliance Magazine*).

And on it goes: situated in the heart of Buckhead in Atlanta, Whirlpool's 12,000 square foot Insperience Store offers visitors fully equipped kitchens and family studios, so they can try out the latest Whirlpool and KitchenAid brand home appliances. Shoppers spend an average of two hours 'smelling the fresh scent of delicate clothing kept ready-to-wear in the Personal Valet Clothes Vitalizing System', 'touching the chilled interior of a Polara range, feeling how it will keep food cool up to 24 hours until a preset cooking time' and 'turning up the heat on a high-powered cooktop'. According to the company, 90 per cent of visitors buy a Whirlpool appliance (Source: *Washington Post*).

So, are you trying hard enough? Are you constantly thinking of innovative ways to get shoppers to try your product?

10 REstoring your ethics – how to succeed by being ethical

There's much talk around the world about companies becoming more ethical. Nowhere is this more important than retail – the point of contact with your ultimate consumer... the shopper.

> We don't do things to be good. Green is green (the colour of the US dollar).
> Jeffrey Immelt, CEO, General Electric

There's an increasing need to demonstrate your true values in practice these days. Shoppers demand it. The world demands it.

'These people must be very fat', Wang, the daughter of cotton farmers, said during a break. Like most Chinese factory workers she is paid by the piece, less than a penny for every pair of boots she stitches, small or large (IHT, 2006f).

Low wages at tens of thousands of factories across China have fuelled fears in the United States and Europe that Western manufacturing industries are being decimated by cheap exports. US and European officials argue that factories like these, relatively unencumbered by regulation and sheltered by an undervalued currency, give China an unfair advantage. But as the world is beginning to discover, a close-up look at these factories shows a different picture, one of vulnerability and tiny margins on the Chinese side.

The biggest earnings in the mass manufacturing business, according to factory owners and other industry executives, both foreign and Chinese, are not made by the companies producing the shoes, but by those who market and sell them in the United States and Europe. The manufacturing process of a boot begins with a smooth piece of leather imported from the United States. After 155 laborious steps, it becomes a flawless pair of tan work boots. The factory, owned in part by a foreign investor, sells each pair for $15.30, from which it earns a pre-tax profit of about 65 cents. A major US retailer, after factoring in shipping, store rent and salaries, sells the boots for $49.99. Assuming a pre-tax profit margin of about 7 per cent, an average among large US retailers, it earns $3.46 on the same pair of boots. Although they are tagged 'Made in China', by the time they sell for $49.99, the $15.30 boots generate twice as much wealth in the United States as they do in China. Of the roughly $46.50 the US retailer spends to get the boots to market, at least $29 circulates entirely within the United States, paying the salaries of advertisers, website designers, truckers and salespeople.

Steve Feniger, a manufacturing expert in Hong Kong who has spent 27 years obtaining goods from China, says the threefold mark-up by the US retailer that buys all the Tianjin factory's work boots is rather low, compared with that for products that carry well-known brand names.

'If you took Calvin Klein jeans it would be more like four or five times', said Feniger, who is managing director of SSPartners, a trading company, and who previously ran factories making products for Warnaco Group, which owns such brands as Calvin Klein, Nautica and Chaps. A Ralph Lauren polo shirt, Feniger said, is made in China for about $3.50 and then sold in the United States for $30.

'The power is very much with the buyer rather than the seller', he said. 'It's a hard and lonely job being at the manufacturing end of the industry.' A decade ago the typical profit margin for Chinese shoe and garment factories was about 10 per cent. Now they are very lucky to get 5 per cent, factory owners and economists say.

James Kynge, a British expert on the Chinese economy, calculates that Chinese factory workers earn less in real terms, on average, than Britons did during the Industrial Revolution. The amount that the Tianjin factory workers receive is so small that if every salary in the factory were doubled, the final shelf price in a US retail outlet would increase from $49.99 to $51.

Rising costs in China may ultimately cut into the profit margins of retailers like Wal-Mart, as well as companies that obtain their products in China, like Timberland or Nike. But the short-term impact on retail prices is likely to be negligible.

Why does all this matter? Well, it increasingly does. People and therefore shoppers are increasingly concerned about these types of exploitation. And they are making moves to counter it. The fastest-growing section of the coffee market worldwide is Fairtrade coffee, which guarantees (in theory) the producers a price that is fair, albeit at an inflated price to the consumer. Shoppers increasingly boycott products of questionable production origin, whether they be celebrity-endorsed sneakers or upmarket luxury goods. In fact, the fastest-growing athletic sneaker in the United States is still celebrity endorsed – but with a difference. It happens to be very low priced and affordable.

You can be ethical with anything. Innocent Drinks in the UK is a brand that's not only the third fastest-growing company in the UK, but one of its most ethical. Innocent has always been in the ethics game – long before it became commercially desirable. Innocent also gives away drinks to the homeless, plants trees, encourages recycling and donates to the developing world, while its entire staff are treated to a snow-boarding trip every year, awarded £2,000 for the birth of each child and invited to apply for a £1,000 scholarship to achieve something they've always wanted to do. But when pushed on the motives of Innocent's almost utopian approach to business, they insist they're very suspicious of 'corporate social responsibility' and the partners are simply working in a way they think is right. 'We do these things because we want to and because we can, not for any other reason', says Richard Reed, one of Innocent's founders. 'I don't want to be judged as good for doing this stuff on the side. I want to be judged on making the world a tiny bit better by making juices people like and doing it in as socially and environmentally friendly a way as possible. And if we give some of our profits to people that are less blessed than we are, it's because we can and want to.' Probably a healthy way of viewing the situation.

You can see this return to ethics retailing very clearly in the UK grocery market, where Britain's supermarkets are falling over themselves to prove their environmental credentials. The UK's biggest grocery retailers are stressing their green and environmental credentials to an ever more sophisticated and cynical shopper (*Sunday Times*, 2006b).

Cynics might suggest that the retailers are merely trying to cash in on growing demand from customers. But whatever their motives, the trend is changing the face of our food giants and the thousands of companies that supply them.

Initiatives have been tumbling out of the food and retail sector, ranging from wholesale changes in the way food is packaged or transported to more offbeat schemes. There has certainly been a change in buying habits. A report on ethical consumerism published by the Co-operative Bank showed that spending on 'ethical' food, including organics and Fairtrade, was a little more than £4 billion (US $8 billion) in 2004, up from £3.8 billion in 2003.

> There is a new moral or social dimension to the market.
> Professor Jeremy Moon of Nottingham University Business School
>
> The market has changed over the past two or three years. In the past, the market was driven by price. But so much value has been stripped out by going down the price route, customers have cottoned on to that.
> Steven Esom, managing director of Waitrose

The drive by the nation's largest grocers to enhance their record on environmental issues is having a knock-on effect on their brand suppliers. Some multinational food companies such as Pepsico, owner of Walkers crisps, are more focused on making their products healthier, while many suppliers are working in tandem with retailers to improve recycling and energy-efficiency targets.

Here are some specific changes being implemented.

Tesco

- Cutting carrier bags by 25 per cent in two years. All bags to become biodegradable.
- Will reduce deliveries to stores to cut congestion and make deliveries quieter.
- Wants to introduce regional counters in stores to promote local produce. Will host open days for regional producers to meet buyers.

Asda

- Plans to have no waste going to landfill sites by 2010.
- Introducing biodegradable packaging on organic food by spring 2007.
- Increased use of biodiesel fuel in its transport fleet; 5 per cent of fuel used is biofuel.

J Sainsbury

- All ready meals to move to compostable packaging.
- Intends to install state-of-the-art recycling centres.
- Carbon emissions from its sites reduced by 20 per cent since 2000.
- Has set target to source 70 per cent of organic food that can be grown in the UK to come from the UK.

Waitrose

- Strong commitment to sourcing fish from sustainable sources.
- No GM ingredients in any own-branded food products. Please note, United States.
- Trying out scheme to allow local suppliers to deliver goods directly to stores.

Marks & Spencer

- All coffee and tea sold is Fairtrade, as is all tea and coffee at in-store restaurants and staff canteens.
- All food made with non-GM ingredients and using only free-range eggs.
- Rated as best UK retailer on supporting sustainable fishing by Marine Conservation Society and Greenpeace.
- Using between 30 per cent and 50 per cent recycled plastic in smoothie bottles and salad packs.

Ethics is here to stay. Let's be clear about that. Why not make it part of your retail make-up. Show you're actually doing something good for all and try to involve the community in a straightforward way. The flagship is a key aspect of this, where you can truly suggest that ethics is part of your corporate drive.

Ethics is a force that's here to stay. Make sure it becomes an integral part of your retail efforts.

Well, are you REobsessed with the future imperatives for brands in retail environments? Have you started to REsolve the big squeeze by getting significantly closer to your shopper by mastering the shopping experience? Have you REassessed and REconnected with them? The first stage should be the REstorming of future plans to ensure your retail efforts are in tune with the actionable, relevant trends of today. This new direction then needs the power of REcreative energy, a REstormed energy that will focus your overall efforts for future success.

We go on from here to look at brands that have succeeded and try to understand why.

Part 2

How to succeed by winning

11 The companies doing it right

Learning from the winners

There's nothing to winning, really. That is, if you happen to be blessed with a keen eye, an agile mind, and no scruples whatsoever.

Alfred Hitchcock (1899–1980)

It's worth pausing in our hectic lives to ask ourselves who has been successful in the world of retail and why? Which are the world's best retail brands?

How do you select them? And just what are the features of their business that make them so successful? Is there a formula for success that we can learn from?

When we say retail, we are referring to all brands that seek to sell their products. We of course include traditional retailers as well as brands that have made retail an increasing part of the focus of their activities. The definition of retail is selling goods. That is as applicable to a mass market retailer who sells manufacturers' brands as it is to an upmarket fashion boutique as it is to selling airline tickets on the web. The point is we're selling something. Therefore we're in the business of retail. We are all in the business of retail, be it a classic retailer or an FMCG brand. Retail is about selling and winning at selling is indeed the business we are all in. We should all look to become a retail winner.

Who would you rather be?

Nike with its ever-expanding and increasingly successful concept stores; Apple with its revolutionary flagship stores that have reversed the Apple story of decline and helped explode the sales of their ubiquitous iPod; P&G which claims to spend the same marketing budget as four years ago, but which believes it is four times more effective with its communications as a result of its in-store marketing; Tesco which has revolutionized the concept of mass selling in the UK with its belief that it can eventually sell you anything you might need in your life, from food to drugs to a mortgage; or finally Selfridges with its revolutionary store in Birmingham in the UK which has dragged the department store concept screaming into the 21st century.

Who would you rather not be?

Hewlett-Packard with a retail strategy (until recently) stuck unconvincingly between Dell computers' dynamic direct selling systems and Apple's revolutionary flagship stores; Compaq in the United States which dominates cable, but finds it increasingly difficult to communicate its advantages in the fragmented media universe it helped create; LEGO which faces bankruptcy as it tries to move from an outdated view of how to sell and how to manufacture; Marks & Spencer which arguably continues to be stuck in the 60s, while constantly disillusioning its traditional core target audience of 40+-year-olds; or finally Sony which seems to be getting everything wrong these days, from recalled batteries to delayed PlayStation 3 launches that fail to give shoppers what they really want, when they want it.

The choice is yours!

This is the future and it's not going to go away. The game is up! The world is full of companies failing to realize their retail ambitions. Often the primary limiting factor is their ability to deal with the increasing power of the mass retailers. Whole industries are in danger of being decimated as fewer and fewer companies have the strength or knowledge to flex their muscles. The moment of truth for you! Are you ready to be a retail winner? Start getting ready to win or lose. Retail at the point of action is the smartest and hottest ticket in town. You have to get yourself ready for the Retail game: building sales by creating brands from the shelf and out. It's increasingly critical to understand that the purchase point of action is your prime and absolutely most important choice of media. Retail is the ultimate expression of your brand values. You need to fulfil brand promises instead of simply communicating them. If you can't manifest your brand this way, you're simply not realizing your complete potential.

Do you have a brand image that's good? Is the strength of that image reflected in what you achieve at retail? Surprisingly, it often is not. There are three major brands shown in Figure 11.1. Only one – Apple – can manage both. That's why it's such a success. That's why its sales, image and share price continue to grow, let alone its profit.

We've forgotten how to sell!

Let us repeat our mantra we believe in for companies' business philosophy: we create sale(s).

Today, brands are squeezed by retailers, private labels, media and shoppers. Brands need to reconnect with their shoppers. Brands need to move from a focus on brand awareness to a focus on brand selection.

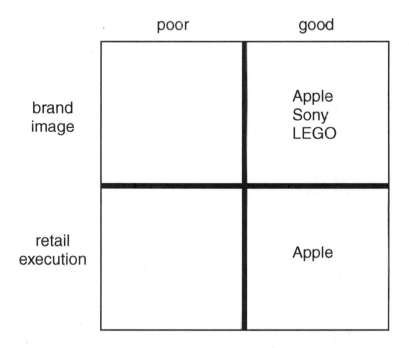

Figure 11.1 Image vs execution grid

Successful brands in the future will be those with relevant new actionable shopper insights. We need to spend our efforts re-obsessing about a company's prime objective – creating sale(s).

Retail is fundamentally critical because no matter how hard you work at developing products there's little point if you can't sell them to your ultimate consumer. The world in most instances has forgotten this simple truism. We have been obsessed with the latest gizmo, the latest fashion, the latest trend and the latest ad. This is almost used as an excuse for not getting to grips with the problem that faces people every day they walk into their companies: how do I sell what I made or bought yesterday? Most organizations often don't need to change their product – but they do need to change the way they sell them. This is not about hiring more salesmen – it's about changing your total philosophy and total way of doing things. In reality, most organizations do a very bad job of selling, a job that is going to become increasingly difficult as the retailers gain more and more power... and choose to exert it.

Let's show you why!
Let's show you how!
Let's show you who!

12 Becoming a retail phenomenon

How to become a retail winner

> If winning isn't everything, why do they keep score?
>
> Vince Lombardi (1913–70)

So is there an elite list of retail winners? And what links the members of this elite group of retail winners? Do they share ways of doing business that have propelled them to the top? Can we learn anything from their case histories? Is there a recipe for launching a product and creating a retail and cultural phenomenon? We believe the answer is yes!

We believe – and these case studies show – that there are distinct yet connected ingredients that are critical to the successful generation of a retail brand icon. We believe these ingredients act as an analytical tool to help us understand our position and potential that much better. This checklist with its 'magic' ingredients can act as a framework for you to check your position and potential. We would now invite you to check your position against each of these criteria. We do not pretend to give any ultimate answers – we merely point out the preferred route to success. Having examined literally hundreds of case studies in the past three years, we have isolated 25 that we believe demand more attention... 25 case studies that show you some ways forward. Yes, you may know others and possibly better ones. But these 25 cases show clearly what can be done if you allow your brand to become retail obsessed and if you pursue a strategy for winning. We believe it's a very useful exercise to pause and reflect on their actions.

A unique global analysis of the brands that are truly succeeding at retail

The analysis of who's winning at retail is based on a unique global study which was first realized in the book *Retailization*. Three years in the making, *Retailization* tells the real story (for the first time) of what it takes to survive as a brand these days in an increasingly unbalanced commercial world. *Retailization* shows that the brand world is literally out of control in the multi trillion dollar global world of retailers. It's not what you sell these days that's important, it's if you can or are allowed to sell it.

But it's not just the survivors we're interested in. Over the course of three years we have researched literally hundreds of brands around the world in an effort to identify the ones that stand out and make a difference at retail. The ones that have not been content with just being an image... but which have gone out of their way to sell themselves and to excel in their retail efforts. This section of the book is dedicated to those brands. We explain why they're successful and why they can make a difference. You too can learn from these cases, whether it's the case of P&G, a global giant, or Yoyamart, a one-shop phenomenon.

The role of retailization?

We've come this far... it's about time we clearly defined retailization. The simple definition is optimizing sale(s) by connecting brands to shoppers through the power of retail thinking. How do we do this? Simply put, we optimize the value of the brand at all the points of contact it has with the retail world. We start by imagining the brand as a source of light. Traditionally, that source of light has been pointed towards our consumer, with an objective of building brand preference and ultimately purchase. However, this objective has become increasingly meaningless as the power of mass communications has fragmented and eroded and the ultimate consumer has developed from a passive consumer watching television to an active shopper seeking the best they can get. Our mission is to help the brand provide the shopper with just that – the best products bought in the best possible way. Our main tools are to use the very things that squeeze today's brand and turn them to our brand's advantage: to make brand selection a reality; to realize a sale or even more importantly sales. To realize the full retail potential of your brand, use the key points of retail contact that a brand touches as a catalyst to restore and recharge the brand energy that has long been drained from it. We use those key points of contact as a way of focusing our thinking and subsequent actions. The retail points of contact are in essence lenses, which allow us to refocus our brand energy, REigniting a new more powerful brand – a retailized brand – a brand that unsqueezes the squeeze (Figure 12.1).

You must confront the new reality of the squeezed brand, the new reality of the age of the retailer. The key is to think like a retailer and brand from the shelf and out. It's a whole new ball game out there, with new rules, new tactics and new tools. You can do all the conventional marketing in the

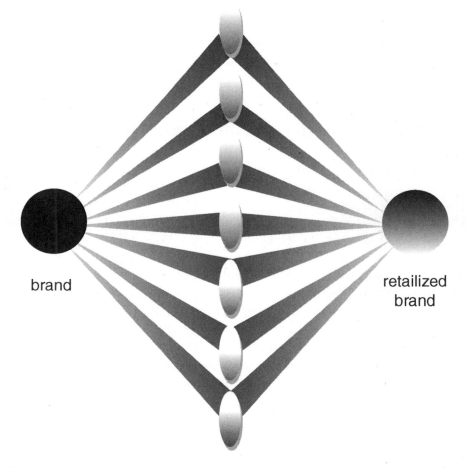

brand   retailized
                                         brand

Figure 12.1 The retailized brand

world, but it's not going to guarantee your survival. You must rethink and potentially reverse your conventional ways of thinking about the world. Reverse the brand thinking, marketing and spending patterns that you have traditionally taken for granted. Marketing as we know it is being severely challenged, and there is an overwhelming need for new communications formulas. It needs redefining. Like a retailer, you need to find ways to encourage purchase and trial at the point of action. You have to focus on that point of action… the point where shoppers really get involved… the point of brand selection. Even your products may need to be rethought through to maximize their impact in the new retail environments that face us. Finally, your entire organization needs to be retailized to bring out the best from your retail strategies. Fresh thinking. New perspectives. New actions.

The shelf from where you sell must become the most powerful pivotal force in your world. The very concept of the brand is transforming – from branding to the shelf to branding from the shelf. This is where the action increasingly takes place. This is the arena you must master. It's critical for you to restructure, re-imagine and rethink your entire business and your marketing efforts around that shelf – whether that shelf is in a supermarket or a high-street store, at a trade fair, on the internet or at a shopping mall.

How to identify a winner

REthinking, REimagining and REstructuring brands in the era of retail and shopper power

There are arguably three prime mindsets that determine your winning capability. Starting with the REthink mindset, we cover the first three stages where we need insights and breakthrough research to help us fully understand the shelves we operate on, the competitive framework we compete with and finally the way our shopper interacts with our products.

Once we've understood, we need to start REimagining – start creating. Specifically, that means getting our product concepts retail-centric and our retail impacts as effective as possible.

Finally, we need to do things: we need to REstructure – activate our business. We need to create the communities to drive shoppers to our retail operations. We need to create communities that can feed on the impact created during the shopping experience, communities that can grow and constantly relate to our ambitions. But none of this will work unless we activate everyone in our organizations, activate them to live and breathe retail everyday. You may believe you are already covering all these stages –

we doubt it! Most organizations do one or two of them and fail to link them. You must not only thoroughly complete them all to reach retail heaven, but you must embrace RETAILIZATION as the guiding philosophy to take you along the pathway.

We are living in a world where everyone searches for the next sale. Retail is fundamentally critical because no matter how hard you work at developing products, there's little point if you can't sell them to your ultimate consumer. In order to assess our list of candidates we've put together a simple assessment grid which captures the salient features of the retail brand and scores each brand in turn. We've grouped the key points of contact of retailization into the three phases which we believe any retail brand must encompass (Table 12.1). The ultimate retail brand scores a maximum score of 100. Let's look at our cases one by one.

Table 12.1 Assessment grid

	comments	score (%)
REthink		
REimagine		
REstructure		
RETAILIZATION		

Our winners analysis

Who are the winners? Here's our list of candidates (Table 12.2). Let's look at them one by one. Let's see who really is succeeding at retail and why. Case by case.

Yoyamart: a brand that understands the situation

> We want to make shopping fun for kids and their parents, but especially dads, because they often get bored.
>
> Gena and Stephane Gerbier, Yoyamart.com

Retail brands should deal with 'situiduals', not individuals. An important reason why traditional retailing is problematic is that lack of time is making us all less predictable and less easy to pigeon-hole into convenient definitions. We

Table 12.2   Our retail winners – who, why and how

Retail brand winner	Winning strategy
Yoyamart	a brand that understands the situation
Gooh!	reinventing the boring!
Innocent	an innocent product from an innocent company
Holland & Holland	making more of more
REI	living the brand experience
Dyson	radical innovation
Zara	react rather than predict
Bose	try, try and try again
Tchibo	creating an unchallenged 'star'
Oliviers and Co.	creating wants, not needs
Apple	merging buying with trying
easyJet	creating choice where there's no choice
Red Bull	rewriting the rules
Procter & Gamble	the moments of truth
Gillette	constant innovation
ASSA ABLOY	solve a problem
Peroni	challenging perceptions
H&M	four seconds to get them!
Courvoisier	REvitalization
Senseo	brand co-creation
Guinness	changing the shelf
Starbucks	being in the people-first business
Superquinn	making customers a part of the family
Whole Foods Market	ethics in action
Karmaloop	turning shoppers into fanatics

compromise our given profiles continuously in the search for convenience and quick solutions. We have less and less time and more and more choices. In our frenzied lives, do we have the time to really be individuals, or do we simply respond to the specific situation we are in during our shopping moments, whatever our demographics, loyalties or preferences? Traditional consumer segmentation often provides a very static image of your shoppers, which limits your ability to create unique and relevant shopping experiences. Shoppers continuously zap between lifestyles and situations. So how can we get to them?

This line of thinking allows you to forget about a shopper's history and instead focus on a shopper's present, the situation that he or she is in right now. The only thing that counts is not who is in your shop or in a shop buying your brand, but what binds everybody together as shoppers in that given shopping situation. 'Situations' are proving to be the new focal point. The Copenhagen Institute for Future Sciences has embraced this new development and launched its own theory on the matter. Its findings conclude that we have moved away from the notion of the individual towards the 'situidual'. The 'situidual' is defined as someone with a floating situation-defined identity. This makes complete sense. We live in a world of lifestyle zapping. At times we are snowboarders, the next we are caring and attentive dads, then we are cut-throat businessmen, and sometimes we are even a beer-drinker's companions. We are constantly changing lifestyles, redefining ourselves in a matter of minutes. The result is a constantly changing shopper. But is this really a new phenomenon? We think not. What is new is that we are starting to notice it. Then we need to ask ourselves why so few retailers, brands and marketers are embracing this clearly identifiable opportunity.

Here is a situation you might recognize: career-obsessed and overworked dads on guilt-induced trips to spend quality shopping time with their kids, while their mothers are enjoying some time on their own. Men have a rough time when it comes to shopping for kids. Especially if they're divorced, which is increasingly becoming the norm everywhere. But dads need look no further. The retailer Yoyamart spotted this situation and took care of it. Its answer has been a hip urban dad-friendly store that carries kids' clothing and funky gadgets for dads in a male-centric shopping environment – an environment where dads and kids can spend quality time together.

Yoyamart has turned the shopping experience into a unique centre to cater for this very specific need – dads spending quality shopping time with their kids. Boutiques all over New York cater to mothers, but none are specifically dad-driven. Yoyamart (15 Gansevoort St at Hudson St, NY) sells gizmos, CDs, DVDs, books, toys and other cool kids' gear that dads will love. Products include a centric-safe kid's seat that attaches to the crossbar of a man's bike. For investment bankers with the best taste (and funds to match), the new Torck stroller, imported from Belgium, is designed to rival the popular SUV-style Bugaboo. Those on a tighter budget will appreciate snazzy child-sized Ray-Ban sunglasses. Also look for togs for 2- to 12-year-olds and funky footwear, including Moon Boots. The store features Japanese robot toys and gadgets, cushions shaped like Andy Warhol's banana from 'The Velvet Underground and Nico' album cover, and apparel and footwear by fashionable brands, such as Puma and Diesel, as well as a big-screen TV and a DVD and CD selection designed to please cool fathers.

Two couples – Gena and Stephane Gerbier, and Cristina and J D Boujnah, created Yoyamart. They opened Yoya in 2002, and later expanded the baby boutique to include designer children's furniture. In 2004, the couples opened Yoyamart, which caters to older children and their parents, especially dads. The store has been described as 'designed for fathers by fathers', and this indeed was part of the goal.

Their latest innovative offering is art chocolate bars. Yoyamart introduced a full line of gourmet choc-o-graphic Artist Bars featuring labels from 10 artists, including Gary Baseman, Nathan Jurevicious, David Horvath, Sun-Min Kim, Rolito, Toy2R, Friends With You, Tim Biskup, Dalek and J D Boujnah. A portion of the sales of Artist Bars is donated to children's art education efforts. The bar flavours include Milk Chocolate, Bittersweet, Crispy Rice, Dark Chocolate with Almonds, Dark Chocolate with Mint, Milk Chocolate with Hazelnuts, Dark Chocolate Espresso and the boutique's old favourite Salty Pretzel.

First understand the situation

So what have Yoyamart got right? First, they have demonstrated an excellent understanding of the shopper and the need for a unique shopping situation (Table 12.3). They have created a new unique shelf for a rapidly expanding market. They have backed this up with an innovative product range, well presented. When it comes to scoring its retailization efficiency, the brand does particularly well in the REthink and RE-imagine phases. Time will determine their future success in the REstructure phase as they further expand their brand and operations.

Table 12.3   Yoyamart

YOYAMART	comments	score (%)
REthink	excellent understanding of the shopper	70
REimagine	innovative product range well presented	50
REstructure	still developing	50
RETAILIZATION	**understanding the situation**	63

Gooh! Reinventing the boring!

Good food to go...

Anything can be reinvented, especially the boring. And what's more boring than fast food? Or worse-tasting? But now you can have good fast food and it's called GOOH. What on earth can drive a company to call

Add soft drinks, smoothies, fresh fruit salad and desserts direct from Operakällaren and you have a complete dinner to take home
Ari Raudasvirta, Commercial Manager of Arlanda Schiphol Development Company (ASDC)

itself Gooh!? A new fast food chain called Gooh! has opened up its first stores in Stockholm, promising great tasting food to go. To go. Gooh. The idea is to sell really good ready meals to people on the move – to bring home for dinner or to work for lunch. This concept is actually not very common in Stockholm; either you have to go to a restaurant to pick up a ready meal or buy something boring and fatty at the grocery store. GOOH is apparently an internet abbreviation for Get Out Of Here. Hence Gooh! This new gourmet take-away food concept is a joint venture between the legendary Stockholm restaurant Operakällaren and Cerealia Foods, part of the giant Swedish farmer-owned cooperative Lantmännen. The concept is based on offering tasty, healthy take-away food prepared according to Operakällaren's recipes.

The first shop opened in September 2005 on Norrlandsgatan in Stockholm and has become a major success in a short period. In February 2006, Gooh! opened a shop in SkyCity at Stockholm's Arlanda airport.

'The new concept is now expanding at a rapid pace, with four new shops, and we are very pleased that Arlanda will be getting one of them. This new shop is consistent with our strategy of strengthening and updating the choice of good food in SkyCity. Gooh! is an alternative that provides good value for money and is a supplement to Arlanda's restaurants', says Ari Raudasvirta, Commercial Manager of Arlanda Schiphol Development Company (ASDC), which develops shops and restaurants at the airport. Operakällaren's Chef des Cuisines, Stefano Catenacci, has developed dishes that satisfy tastes ranging from Swedish home cooking and Italian pasta dishes to Oriental dishes.

A new idea needs a new technology

In order to serve ready meals from their own recipes Gooh! has had to harness a new packaging technology called MicVac. The principle behind the patented MicVac method is that the producer prepares and pasteurizes the food directly in the consumer packaging using a method-specific valve. Food ingredients (typically 100–500 gram) are inserted into a tray or pouch at the manufacturers' premises and a purpose-designed valve is applied, after which the package is sealed. The package is transported into a tunnel where the product is cooked. The food releases steam, increasing the pressure and opening the valve. A controlled amount of steam is released through the valve together with air from the package. After cooking, the cooling process begins immediately. The valve closes while there is still 'over pressure' in the pack. The remaining steam condenses, causing 'under pressure' in the pack. The final result is a cooked, pasteurized and vacuum-packed product. The chilled consumer pack is put straight into the microwave oven on full power. After 2 to 4 minutes, depending on the dish and the oven, the valve starts to beep to tell the consumer that the food is hot enough to eat. It's like whistling for your food.

If you can reinvent fast food you can reinvent anything. Gooh! has created a new unique shelf for a rapidly expanding market by taking quality food into the less prestigious fast-food industry (Table 12.4). They have an interesting innovative product range, well presented, with breakthrough packaging technology. Communications is under development and in need of investment. It will be interesting to see how far the brand can develop in the future, particularly internationally, and who mimics it first. Gooh is a word that should travel, despite some obvious translation concerns, into English. We wonder if anyone told them what Gooh means in Anglo Saxon!!! It will also be interesting to see if they can keep this idea fresh all the time – we think it's critical to constantly change and re-stimulate the offerings on a regular basis.

Table 12.4   Gooh!

GOOH!	comments	score (%)
REthink	old shelf looks new	70
REimagine	well presented and well located	50
REstructure	still developing	50
RETAILIZATION	**reinventing the boring**	63

Innocent Drinks: an innocent product from an innocent company

Those delicious people at Innocent Drinks have announced a new kind of smoothie – a guest smoothie designed by you... the idea with this one is to get fresh ideas out of our kitchen and into the shops as quickly as we can. The first escapee is pineapples, blueberries and ginger. Delicious with subtle hint of ginger malice. Dangerous. So if you have got creative in the kitchen recently with your smoothies then drop them a line at bemyguest@innocentdrinks.co.uk

Innocent Drinks make totally natural tasty little drinks. Their range includes smoothies (100 per cent pure crushed fruit and juices, never from concentrate), thickies (yoghurt, fruit and spices) and juicy waters (natural thirst-quenching drinks made with spring water). Innocent is now the number one smoothie brand and the third fastest-growing company in the UK (*Sunday Times* Fast Track survey, 2006).

Innocent Drinks was born when three disgruntled college friends, eager to step outside the rat race, joined together to start their own business (Interbrands Brand channel.com). To test their idea, the three friends embarked on a unique form of product concept testing. The test site was a London music festival, and the stimuli £500 worth of fruit. Garbage cans were marked 'Yes' and 'No', and a handwritten sign read: 'Do you think we should give up our jobs to make these smoothies?' By the end of the day the 'Yes' bin was overflowing with empties. The following day the founders quit their jobs to start Innocent Drinks. Innocent prides itself on providing natural, pure juice drinks and nothing else. Literally, nothing else – 'No sugar. No water. No concentrates'. The message certainly sounds intriguing, but what really makes the Innocent brand different? The fruity beverage market is already cluttered with strong competitors like Naked in the United States and The Feel Good Drinks Co in the UK. Each brand promises natural, pure and fresh ingredients, and at first glance they look similar. A closer look, however, reveals the difference. At the core of Innocent's success we see words. Simple, honest, fresh words that add up to a powerful statement about the personality of this unique brand. This is a brand that stands for innocence. Innocent drinks are surprisingly cool. The smoothies in small plastic bottles with witty alternative labelling are the drinks to be seen with and at almost £2 ($4) per 250 ml they should be, too. But Innocent is no passing fad, for it has succeeded where virtually every nutritionist has failed: making fruit fun while being healthy.

The idea for Innocent Drinks came from scrutinizing their own hectic urban lifestyles. 'We realized that every time we were going on holiday we'd work like mad beforehand and end up feeling totally knackered. We were all working really long hours and finishing at a time when the only place open to get food was the kebab house and it was too late to be bothered to go to the gym. We realized if there was a small and easy way of doing something healthy that didn't take any time we'd do it and so would our friends.'

The founders insist it was confidence in the product that made them persevere. 'We knew people who got to taste our fresh fruit drinks liked them and wanted them and that retailers were happy to stock them once they saw people wanted them. Every time someone said "no" I just said "why not?" They'd say "it won't work", I'd say "why not?" They'd say "it's too expensive", we'd say "we know there's people who will pay it". It's a case of overcoming each hurdle at a time.'

Their mantra is one certainly borne out by Innocent's early days. Distributors initially refused to stock the drinks, so one Bank Holiday weekend they loaded up a van and took the drinks round delicatessens and health shops in Notting Hill themselves. 'We just said "we're a local juice company that's just started up, here's four boxes for free, stick them on your shelves and if they sell give us a ring".' Over that first weekend Innocent drinks made it into 50 shops and were an immediate success, with 45 wanting more. 'We went back to the distributors and said "these companies want them", and gave them a pallet for free.' Five years on and 10 million sales later, Innocent drinks are in shops across the country and word is spreading. Now when you go into Sainsbury's, for example, they are sometimes the only smoothies brand on the shelf, positioned alongside the orange juice offerings from Sainsbury's private label. Sainsbury's must truly believe they offer something else.

But despite the overwhelming growth, until recently Innocent hadn't spent a penny on advertising. Innocent's competitors use fun language in their product names (for example, Odwalla's Mo'Beta and AntioxiDance), while its own products are flavour focused, plain and descriptive. In the smoothies line we see 'blackberries and blueberries' and 'strawberries and bananas', which sound rather mundane when you consider Naked's Zenergy or Odwalla's Vanilla Al'Mondo. Innocent's distinctive voice, however, is more subtle and nuanced. The ingredient list on the side of an Innocent drink, for example, might include 'a few small pebbles' hidden among the crushed strawberries and mashed bananas. It is only when you reach the bottom of the list that you find: 'We lied about the pebbles.'

The website also takes a simple but powerful approach to words and writing style. A link to Innocent's online gym is titled 'I'm fat. Let me in.' However, distancing itself from the corporates is something Innocent seems to spend a lot of effort maintaining. Its witty packaging, with ditties such as 'separation occurs, but mummy still loves daddy', Fruit Towers premises, grass-covered vans and cow-patterned carts, provides a cool alternative image that in a world increasingly disillusioned with Americanization and corporate power is perhaps as effective a marketing ploy as any other.

We like to keep things fresh, whether that is our marketing or what goes in the bottle. Whilst we do take the drinks seriously, we have a bit of fun too, so you might see our delivery vans covered in grass up and down the UK, or read our labels which just chat about what is going on in the office. We encourage people to call the banana phone and tell us what they think, or pop into Fruit Towers. By remaining open to the most important people, the ones that drink our drinks, and never compromising on quality we hope we can keep offering people the best drinks on the market.

Adam Balon, Chief Squeezer, Innocent Drinks

We talked about the need to REstore your ethics earlier. Innocent has always been in the ethics game – long before it became commercially desirable.

Recently the company published a book called *Stay Healthy. Be Lazy.* Consistent with its overall voice, the book sets an honest straightforward tone. 'Are you lazy?' asks the book. 'Great, that makes two of us. But that shouldn't stop us from being healthy. By incorporating a few of the simple habits contained in the book, you can live a contented, healthy life whilst still having enough time to be lazy and eat the odd plate of chips.'

The simple, friendly approach translates across key brand touch-points. The company's unique 'cow vans', complete with horns, eyelashes, udders and a tail, are assigned personalities and even bios. The product packaging is also a clever representation of the brand. Unlike its fellow beverages, Innocent is simple and rather muted. The bottle is clear, with a simple product information band in one colour. The product stands out precisely because it is so different from the other loudly colourful beverages on the shelf. When a product has become a retail success it's important to stick to your roots and preserve what you were and what you meant to be.

You don't get much more saturated than the drinks market, so we take our hats off to Innocent's success. Where others have tried and failed to compete with or copy Coke, Innocent just succeeded. They have a 'makes sense, feels good' proposition combined with a quirky positioning. This is a powerful combination for a simple beverage and a real coup in a competitive market.

The brand is all about feeling good, whether you really believe it or not. The name is great, the product is delicious, the advertising and the irreverent copy on the packaging go straight to the point. So what of the future? They have dreams of expanding Innocent's brand across other healthy sectors and can see a day when there are Innocent baby products, Innocent body care and even an Innocent island. But if Innocent does grow up into a multi-product company, could it maintain the identity it's so carefully created?

> The smoothie market is growing at a phenomenal rate and Innocent has grown 60 per cent each year we've been in business. This is because we make the best drinks on the market, and also because they are tapping into a real consumer demand for products that are natural, convenient and healthy. If you think about government initiatives to eat more fruit & veg, rising gym membership, concern with what goes into your food, these are all very real trends that are having an impact on how healthy and food conscious our nation is. On the whole, fresh, healthy convenience food is on the up. Looking at your local store a few years ago, you would never have expected to find fresh fruit or veg in

> there – just tins & cleaning things. Now everyone is offering healthier, fresher options because that is what consumers are looking for.
>
> Adam Balon, Chief Squeezer, Innocent Drinks

Clearly this is a company in a hurry to grow. But also a company that wants to retain its original mission come what may. It's that obsession that makes Innocent a great retail brand. Innocent have clearly demonstrated an excellent understanding of the shopper and the need for increasingly healthy products, creating a new unique shelf for a rapidly expanding market. They have an interesting innovative product range, well presented. Excellent cheap communications have given the brand a real buzz (Table 12.5).

Finally, they were recently described as the second-best employer to work for in the UK by Marketing Week/Michael Page's Marketing Top Employer Survey, after Virgin. As Innocent marketing controller Heather Callin put it, 'the energy, pace and passion gives you excitement. It is small enough to make a difference and you can see the effects of your product innovation and advertising in a very short timescale.' She says that large companies often lack this immediacy (*Marketing Week*, 2006).

Table 12.5   Innocent

INNOCENT	comments	score (%)
REthink	excellent understanding of the shopper and health trends	80
REimagine	innovative product range imaginatively presented	80
REstructure	real buzz	70
RETAILIZATION	**staying innocent**	77

Holland & Holland: making more of more

> Holland & Holland is a universe of its own. A universe of refinement and ultimate luxury. A universe offering its very privileged clients the comfort of the most exquisite materials, soft and resistant, and the excellence of the most innovative techniques, allowing you to brave the most extreme climates. The Holland & Holland universe, at the same time rare and exceptional, comfortable, handy and exclusive, which we invite you to discover and enjoy.
>
> Marie Streichenberger, Artistic Director, Holland and Holland.com

A product can possess endless possibilities of relevant, sellable add-on features. You should always strive to make it into more – more than just that one product. The scope of the product should be bigger than the product itself. You should make more of more. An interesting example of this is UK company Holland & Holland, one of the world's leading sporting gun and rifle makers. The firm was founded by Harris Holland (1806–96) in 1835. Although accounts of his background are somewhat sketchy, it is believed that his father was an organ builder, while Harris had a tobacco wholesale business in London.

Obviously he was successful, as he was often seen at various pigeon shoots at important London clubs, as well as leasing a grouse moor in Yorkshire (Holland and Holland.com). Being a very accomplished shot, his friends convinced him to start his own gun-making business. It presently produces around 100 handmade guns a year. Depending on the model of gun, each one takes between 650 and 1,250 hours to manufacture. No part of a Holland & Holland gun is interchangeable, it is always particular to each gun, down to the smallest pin. With this level of attention, it is no surprise that Holland & Holland is considered to make some of the best guns in the world.

The sheer exclusivity and luxury potential of the brand was one of the main reasons that fashion brand Chanel decided to purchase Holland & Holland. It also decided to make it more. Chanel has started leveraging the gun-making business into numerous Holland & Holland accessories such as hunting clothing, luxury men's and women's clothing, cufflinks, garters, jewellery and so on – fully realizing the retail potential. Holland & Holland has started on a programme of major expansion. An exclusive line of clothing and accessories has been introduced, both for the shooting public and for discerning ladies and gentlemen to combine quality and fashion. New stores have been opened in Paris on Avenue Victor Hugo, in New York at 10 East 40th Street, Suite 1910, in Harrods and in London's Heathrow Terminal 3, while the London flagship store at 31–33 Bruton Street has been completely renovated and expanded. The Shooting Grounds in Northwood have also been beautifully modernized. They celebrated their 165th anniversary in the year 2000!

So how do they score? They have leveraged the highest-quality products into new retail opportunities with traditional but imaginative product developments (Table 12.6). Their organization is still under development with Chanel's backing. If you turn your product into more, you will not only increase sale(s), you will probably also enhance the chances of shopper loyalty, as the product franchise offers more possibilities of fresh, new shopping experiences. Always try to make it more!

Table 12.6 Holland & Holland

HOLLAND & HOLLAND	comments	score (%)
REthink	leveraged the highest quality	80
REimagine	traditional, but imaginative	80
REstructure	Chanel backing	50
RETAILIZATION	**making more of more**	70

REI: living the brand experience

> You haven't been shopping until you've visited REI's flagship store!
>
> 10 best.com

REI has been serving Seattleites since 1944. In 1938, mountain climbers Lloyd and Mary Anderson joined with 21 fellow Northwest climbers to found Recreational Equipment, Inc (REI). The group structured REI as a consumer cooperative to purchase high-quality ice axes and climbing equipment from Europe because such gear could not be purchased locally. The word quickly spread, and soon many other outdoors people joined the co-op. As REI grew, so too did the range of outdoor gear available to the co-op members. If you find yourself in Seattle, you should make a point of visiting REI, the outdoor gear and clothing store. It's a place where people love to shop because it is a truly exceptional shopping experience. At REI, you do not wait in line or spend hours hunting down a sales assistant. You simply check in at the appropriate department (for example, skiing or hiking), and when a skiing or hiking expert is ready to give you his or her undivided attention, you will be buzzed. While you are waiting you can try out your climbing skills on a 30-foot wall, be inspired in the travelling department or simply hang out by the fireplace while enjoying a hot cup of chocolate. During the past six decades, REI has grown into a renowned supplier of speciality outdoor gear and clothing. They serve the needs of outdoors people through 82 retail stores in the United States and by direct sales via the internet (REI.com and REI-OUTLET.com), telephone and mail. Today, REI is the United States' largest consumer cooperative, with more than 2.8 million members.

Although the gear sold by REI looks very different now from that sold in 1938, being a cooperative business remains central to REI. While non-members are welcome to shop at REI, only members enjoy special benefits, including an annual member refund on eligible purchases. REI's business success allowed the co-op to return member refunds to its active members in 2005 totalling more than $50 million, and provide $2.5 million in donations in support of the outdoors and outdoor recreation.

REI's reputation is strengthened by an employee team that is recognized both for its knowledge of the outdoors and outdoor equipment and for being a friendly resource in helping any customer, from novice to the highly accomplished, prepare for their outdoor adventures.

10best.com said the following about REI: 'You haven't been shopping until you've visited REI's flagship store! This remarkable outdoor supply store promises an unforgettable experience. They offer an extensive inventory of gear for everything from kayaking to bird watching. Most impressive, however, are the phenomenal facilities, which allow you to assess the merchandise. On-site trails let you test-drive mountain bikes and footwear, a simulated rain room gives you the opportunity to try out a Gore-Tex jacket, and 65-foot pinnacles allow rock climbers to test their gear. You'll also find a great hands-on section for children.'

Patricia Whisler on cityguide.aol.com said: 'The tallest indoor free-standing climbing structure in the world – say that three times fast! At 65 feet high and with more than 1,000 climbing holds, this puppy begs to be tested. REI will provide you with shoes and an expert and you'll even get a certificate saying that you've done the deed. Although REI's Seattle Flagship store has been open for three years and you'd think that everyone and their mother has climbed it, the Pinnacle is still one of the most popular attractions in town. Sign up on the Pinnacle waiting list and you'll be handed a beeper so you can shop to your heart's content while waiting your turn. If you're a member, it won't cost you a thing to climb. Otherwise, be prepared to fork over five bucks. If you're serious about this climbing thing and don't want to wait two hours for a 10-minute romp on this massive rock, inquire with REI about their climbing and belaying classes, led by instructors from the hip Vertical World Climbing Gym in Ballard.'

At REI it's almost unthinkable that you don't get to try out the clothing or gear you are considering buying. You get to try the mountain bike on the trail on the faux mountain that the store is built on or you can try your new hiking shoes on the indoor test course for hiking shoes. You can even go out and try the tent you're considering buying. This is a brand that truly allows you to 'live' it to the full (Table 12.7).

Table 12.7   REI

REI	comments	score (%)
REthink	understood shopper need for involvement and information	80
REimagine	making trial real	80
REstructure	still developing	50
RETAILIZATION	**living the brand**	70

Dyson: radical innovation

In the space of 18 months Dyson became the US market leader with a product that was twice as expensive as the generic market leader who had led the market since its inception.

Often innovation is linked to problem redefinition, that is, looking at a problem in a different way. This allows the designer to have a clear picture of the whole problem and re-evaluate accepted limits. This is perhaps the highest form of innovation.

> A man's reach should exceed his grasp – or what's a heaven for?
> Robert Browning from the poem 'Andrea del Sarto' (1812–89)

One market that thought the physical product was the ultimate solution was the hoovering one. But the market has changed dramatically. The market leader Hoover is now even up for sale... after 98 years as number one. Who said you couldn't change markets very easily? They'd never met James Dyson in action.

How on earth did they achieve this phenomenon? Simply put, they had a great product, brilliantly designed to gain attention. Dyson realized that consumers wanted to see their rubbish as they hoovered, see the effect they were having, and wanted to get rid of those unobtainable dustbin bags that you were increasingly searching for and never had when you really needed them. Retailers literally queued up to stock this product, which turned a boring, plodding sector into one of their most dynamic categories.

Society had accepted the limits of efficiency of conventional vacuum cleaners available to consumers. James Dyson developed a new system for dust extraction and capture which challenged consumers' preconceived ideas of the limits of domestic cleaning appliances. When looking at a Dyson vacuum cleaner one could easily mistake it for a prop from a science fiction movie. It looks awesome. Not only does it look great, it actually represents a category revolution, in a category where nothing really had changed since it was invented. In the United States in particular the brand Hoover had been generic for the category and the clear market leader for 98 years – almost an entire century! Then along came an English brand called Dyson, and in the space of 18 months it became the US market leader with a product that was twice as expensive (Carney, 2005)! Dyson has more or less conquered the world with its great, great products, which are brilliantly designed to gain attention and create involvement. You can actually see your dust being vacuumed, making you feel mighty effective. But the design is not just about looks. Its revolutionary closed-circuit system not only creates a unique, even suction flow, but provides the world with an allergy-safe vacuum cleaner (Natlallergy, 2005). The existing hoover technology apparently sucks for asthmatics as it spews out almost as much dust as it sucks up due to the whole filter system. Dyson tried to come up with a smart way, and succeeded with a closed-circuit system where nothing comes out.

Last, but absolutely not least, the Dyson vacuum cleaner does not use bags! For a long time, people had accepted the limits of the vacuum cleaners available. James Dyson developed a new system for dust extraction and capture which challenged shoppers' preconceived ideas of the limits of domestic cleaning appliances and captured the market! (Table 12.8).

Market leadership was next. His latest innovations are washing machines and hand dryers – areas long overdue for a product design revolution. Dyson is a brand that has let innovation lead it to a better retail future – a retail future where the retailers queue up to stock it. Radical innovation and design has allowed Dyson to upset one of the longest, most entrenched status quo markets in the world. You sometimes have to strive to totally exceed yourself to be truly successful.

Electrolux, the world's largest maker of electrical white goods, dismissed Dyson early on as an idea that wouldn't catch on, when they were offered the opportunity to buy them at an early stage of their development.

Table 12.8   Dyson

DYSON	comments	score (%)
REthink	design that sells	80
REimagine	highly imaginative in a very boring industry	80
REstructure	excellent logistics	70
RETAILIZATION	**radical innovation**	77

Zara: react rather than predict; fashion phenomenally fast

Zara provides freshly baked clothes.
Amancio Ortago Gaona, the founder of Inditex (the owner of Zara)

In the future a lot of fashion brands may have to become mass retailers in their own right. The Spanish fashion brand Zara is a good example of this. Zara are known as the masters of spotting new fashion trends and being able to translate them into products that are affordable phenomenally fast and place them into an environment that's conducive to selling fashionable products at a price that is very mass market. They have established extremely efficient internal systems for bringing products to market at speeds the competition can only dream of. Zara, the fashion retailer, is another exciting example of how to get your whole organization involved in making your company an amazing retalization company.

Design and product development is a highly people-intensive process. Here again Zara is a star. The effort and cost put into product development is becoming more and more questionable when you have no sustainable competitive advantage. The heavy creative workload of 1,000 new styles every month is managed by a design and development team of over 200 people, all based in Spain, and each person in effect produces one or two styles a week. This high cost of product development is more than adequately compensated for by higher realized margins. The entire product development cycle begins from the market research. Zara has made a virtue of short response times. Zara's speed from idea to store is extremely impressive, the objective being to ensure that the stores carry the clothes the shoppers want at the exact time they want them. Zara prides itself on the fact that, within 30 days from identifying a trend, it can have the clothes on the racks. Leaving the competitors confused playing catch-up, Zara excels at an impressive game of being at the forefront of fashion trends, a game that secures better margins and continuous sale(s). Zara's large design team is constantly busy playing the trend-spotting game, churning out more than 1,000 new styles every month. Luckily they are not working entirely on their own. Zara has an insane drive for involving everyone in the trend game, with the goal of staying ahead.

Zara has a rule: react rather than predict. In order to be able to do just this, it involves a good number of people. Zara personnel visit nightclubs and other venues to observe what people are wearing. Zara has open channels to the outside world, allowing anybody to inspire the company and keep it updated on what's hot. At the leading edge of its trend research are the key sales associates and store managers in Zara stores. They are all actively encouraged to observe and engage with customers, sharing ideas and thoughts on trends. They instantaneously report back ideas and thoughts to design headquarters and almost immediately they are converted into new styles and trends. At Zara, every employee is encouraged to be a trend-spotter. There are no focus groups here. Zara's trend identification comes through constant research and interaction. The result is a daily stream of insights by e-mails, pictures and phone calls to design headquarters: insights that Zara's scarily effective production facility quickly transforms into real tangible clothes, ideas that are on the shelves within 30 days (Dutta, 2005).

Zara is riding two of the winning retail trends – being in fashion and low prices – and making a very effective combination out of it (Table 12.9). Zara concentrates on three winning formulas to bake its fresh fashions (Dutta, 2005):

short lead times = more fashionable clothes
lower quantities = scarce supply
more styles = more choice and more chances of getting it right.

Get everybody involved!

Table 12.9   Zara

ZARA	comments	score (%)
REthink	reinvented the fashion concept	90
REimagine	let the shoppers imagination lead the way	90
REstructure	extremely efficient logistics	90
RETAILIZATION	**react rather than predict**	90

Bose: try, try and try again

Bose Corporation was founded in 1964 by Dr Amar G Bose, then professor of electrical engineering at the Massachusetts Institute of Technology. While doing graduate work at MIT in the 1950s, Dr Bose decided to purchase a new stereo system. He was disappointed to find that speakers with impressive technical specifications failed to reproduce the realism of a live performance. This led to extensive research in the fields of speaker design and psychoacoustics – the human perception of sound. Dr Bose's findings resulted in significantly new design concepts that help deliver the emotional impact of live music. The list of major technologies emerging from Bose continues to grow. Fourteen years of research led to the development of acoustic waveguide speaker technology, found in their award-winning Wave® radio, Wave® radio/CD and Acoustic Wave® music systems. Today, you can hear Bose wherever quality sound is important, from the Olympic Games to the Sistine Chapel, from NASA space shuttles to the Japan National Theatre. In the home and on the road, from large outdoor arenas to intimate neighbourhood stores and restaurants, you can hear the realism of the most respected name in sound – Bose; from the latest iPod headphones to iPod dock systems with superior sound.

Product trial does not need to be complicated in our new retail world and can indeed be very exciting. For a long time Bose was known to the world as a maker of superior sound systems. If you wanted great speakers, you bought Bose. However, the company wanted to expand its market and strengthen its position in other areas such as complete home entertainment systems and CD players. Instead of struggling to get onto the shelves and spending fortunes on advertising, it made a deal with its shoppers: Bose offered to send its new Wave Music System to its customers at no charge and let them try the music system for 30 days at no cost. If customers decided against the product, they could return the system to Bose cost free. However, the majority of customers who chose to try the product did not and, on top of that, the activity generated significant word of mouth. Simple! Tryvertising! Creating sale(s) through trial offers endless possibilities of communication (Trendwatching.com reports). As tryvertising is starting to become popular in the real world, it is one of the main drivers of communication in cyberspace. Literally millions of shoppers are sharing their buying and trying experiences with other shoppers. One of the latest initiatives from Bose is a Try & Buy retail kiosk in crowded airports, where frequent flyers about to embark on a noisy flight are likely to give Bose's noise-cancelling headphones a try, if not buy them straight away (Trendwatching.com reports).

Marketers operating in a tryvertising mindset will find completely new 'conversation channels' for their products, if not the most unexpected partners and alliances. As you can tell from the above, tryvertising is more about mindset than science: will you continue to spend the majority of your marketing budget on disliked, message-based advertising, or will you shift considerable amounts of money to a more relevant, empathetic, try-out approach? Tryvertising isn't the old, boring, product sampling – it's trying to make trial the creative and exciting force it should be.

Other Bose initiatives include Bose Information Exchange where members have a platform to voice their opinions about quality sound and great listening experiences, get advance notice of new products, special offers and more. It takes just a few minutes to add the Bose Information Exchange membership to your Bose.com account. It's free and easy. The latest product initiative has been capitalizing on the iPod phenomenon by developing hi-fi units that incorporate the iPod and deliver great sound (Table 12.10).

Table 12.10 Bose

BOSE	comments	score (%)
REthink	invented its own shelf	70
REimagine	consistent use of innovative trial techniques	60
REstructure	generally good	70
RETAILIZATION	**try, try and try again**	67

Tchibo: creating an unchallenged 'star'

'A new experience every week.'

What started off as a branded shop selling coffee has become a major retailer selling key consumer items. Every week Tchibo offers its customers consumer goods – so-called non-food items – under the company's own brand, TCM. Whether the current theme is the kitchen, garden, sport and leisure, clothing or jewellery, the diversity of thematic worlds and the number of articles mean that in the course of a year there is bound to be something for every customer. The composition of weekly thematic worlds is based on ideas that are developed to suit current trends, long before sales get under way. To do this, the product managers concerned monitor developments in the most varied markets from many different perspectives. Important information is supplied on a regular basis through cooperation with trend-spotters and market research companies which analyse long-term developments in society and their influence on shopping habits. This means that Tchibo can adapt to the current desires and needs of its customers, cater for changes in their lifestyle and fulfil their expectations of modern technology.

Products under consideration that match certain criteria in a first stage are then tested in the market in a second stage. Only if this test runs positively – ie is well received by customers – are carefully specified orders sent out. This means that production is exclusively for Tchibo. The quality that customers expect is guaranteed by detailed briefings to manufacturers, as well as tough in-house quality control at Tchibo.

In each case, only one version of each product is offered. Thus, for example, there is only one iron, not 20 from which the customer has to choose. Presented in this way, each item becomes an unchallenged 'star' in the selection. It is important that the various articles on offer in a single phase harmonize and relate to each other. This allows 'A new experience every week' to come into being at Tchibo, mirrored by the window dressing and shop decor, the TCM magazine – detailing the current range, with editorial coverage about the respective phase's theme – a TV schedule and TV commercials.

Tchibo is transformed into a specialist shop, if only briefly. Customers have to act fast, because the offer is purposely limited. This stimulates a 'need', a phenomenon proven by the fact that most purchases are in fact spontaneous.

The history of Tchibo non-food products is closely linked to the history of coffee purchasing. Today's wide range of consumer goods stems from an idea in the 1950s, when coffee was still a real luxury item in Germany and could only be sold in very small quantities. Instead of selling its coffee in the familiar paper bags, Tchibo decided to dispense it in practical sideline products. From then on, customers took their coffee home packed in a kitchen towel or a handkerchief. When larger amounts of coffee could be sold, it was supplied in plastic or tin containers. Customers were pleased to have something they could use again, for storing flour or sugar, for example. Soon Tchibo's orange containers brightened up many a German kitchen. Gradually Tchibo added other new coffee or kitchen-related products to the assortment (Tchibo.com).

What began with a few promotional articles is today an independent, highly professional and creative business unit. The decisive point came in the 1970s when German retailers objected to Tchibo's idea, and in the end the courts put a stop to package offers of that kind. For Tchibo and its customers, this meant that articles could no longer be sold in direct connection with coffee. As a result, the concept was reworked and in 1973, a new, independent product category for non-food articles was created. Initially the range consisted of one or two items, but it soon extended well beyond 'food and drink'. Then, in the mid-1980s, phase sales began, with product offers linked to a central theme that changed every two weeks. Since 1994, phases have changed in a weekly sequence and, through its TCM brand, Tchibo now sells everything – from watches to bicycles to skiwear and saucepans or underwear – that their customers would find useful, practical and desirable. Today, 'a new experience every week' consists of around 15 thematically linked items.

As a complement to shop-based retailing, a mail order company was founded in 1996. All merchandise, as well as coffee, can be ordered by catalogue. Tchibo then made its debut in the tourism business and launched its own travel magazine, *Tchibo Reisen*. What began as a pilot project rapidly developed to include a comprehensive range of holidays. The opening of the first Tchibo shop branch in London in 2000 marked the group's entry into the British market. It's now a major presence on the high streets. Tchibo coffee is also available in Romania. German-speaking Swiss customers join Germany and Austria as the third mail order business segment. The weekly *TCM Magazine* rolls off the press with an editorial about each merchandise theme and a TV programme schedule. It can be picked up in every Tchibo branch. The print-run is around one million.

Tchibo has transformed a simple coffee-bar concept into a dynamic consumer goods retail concept (Table 12.11). By offering a new experience every week they have developed a unique, thriving retail brand experience. A simple FMCG brand has become a retail star in its own right. Why not you?

Table 12.11   Tchibo

TCHIBO	comments	score (%)
REthink	the coffee bar concept transformed	70
REimagine	consistent – a new experience every week	60
REstructure	generally good and becoming international	70
RETAILIZATION	**creating an unchallenged 'star'**	67

Oliviers and Co.: creating wants, not needs

It is through O&CO. that we share and taste the recipes and flavours of the Mediterranean region. In the true spirit of hospitality and generosity, I invite you to discover and savour the authenticity of my beloved homeland.

Olivier Baussan, Founder of O&CO., Oliviersandco.com

Oliviers & Co., a French retail concept, is a chain of stores that has made shoppers spend a great deal of time and money buying olive oil. Shopping for oil been made genuinely fun, interesting and exciting, unlike the supermarket experience which closely resembles a commodity experience. For crying out loud, why can't shoppers just get their olive oil in the supermarket? Because Oliviers & Co. has made it an amazing retail experience to buy olive oil. Shoppers want their mandarin-infused virgin extra or their rich, smooth olive oil soaps. They do not really need it, but they desperately want it. We are in an era of creating wants rather than satisfying needs. This is an essential part of thinking like a retailizer, in order to create profitable sustainable businesses.

About O&CO.

Olivier Baussan, the entrepreneurial son of a journalist and an artist, was inspired by the olive groves surrounding him throughout his childhood in Provence. His adventure began in 1976 when he created L'Occitane, a luxurious line of bath and body goods, featuring hand-crafted shampoos and soaps using plants and essential oils from Provence. Baussan also worked over the years to highlight the olive tree, its fruits and its products. In 1993, he asked 20 photographers from different Mediterranean countries to work freely on the olive tree theme during the course of one year. The result was more than 200 pictures organized into a 1994 exhibit entitled 'The Olive Tree, The gift of the Mediterranean', which was the impetus for O&CO.

Baussan formed O&CO. in 1996 (then called Oliviers & Co) after an extensive tour of the Mediterranean, which only intensified his passion for the olive tree. His first product, a vintage olive oil sampler of eight oils, ultimately led to an expanded line of over 20 distinctive and carefully selected extra virgin olive oils and olive-related products. Baussan opened the first O&CO. store in 1998 on Ile St. Louis in Paris.

O&CO. was born from his passion for the olive tree, olive oils, Mediterranean foods and lifestyle products, with a mission to provide a means for customers to discover the remarkable olive oils and products being produced in the region. O&CO. is a portal for transporting you to this world of sun, sea and olives, and as you taste the various products, you can visit each olive oil's region and learn about the artisans who created them. While olive oils remain the company's core business, the expanded product line includes appetizers, seasonings, biscuits and crackers, pastas and sauces, jams, kitchen accessories and beauty items. With the addition of 60 new products, the company's mission as a Mediterranean Food Merchant is to provide you with a one-stop shopping experience in which you can purchase all the necessary ingredients for a fast, delicious and healthy meal, stock your pantry or purchase gourmet gifts. O&CO. tells the stories of the artisans who give their lives to producing authentic goods and preserving traditions. They currently have 50 stores, including 11 in the United States, located in New York, New Jersey, Boston, Denver, Los Angeles, San Francisco, Newport Beach and Seattle (Table 12.12).

Table 12.12   Oliviers & Co.

Oliviers & Co.	Comments	Score (%)
REthink	leveraged the highest quality by 'turning' wine into oil	80
REimagine	imaginative	70
REstructure	still evolving	50
RETAILIZATION	**creating wants, not needs**	67

The sort of press they receive

The three local branches of the Oliviers chain offer New Yorkers quaint charm to spare, whether in the relatively bucolic West Village, sleek Soho, or the bustling corridors of Grand Central Terminal. Just another mom and pop – that's part of the L'Occitane world empire (outposts on five continents), and one of 50 O&CO.'s in the United States alone. But banish your fears of lowest-common-denominator mass marketing; the rustically decorated shops, outfitted in distressed wood and sunflower gold, are geared to the ample gustatory pleasures of the Mediterranean, primarily olive oil. The high-quality extra-virgins hail from Italy, France, Greece, Spain, and Lebanon, and come in tins for everyday use, as Grand Crus for salads and dipping, and in specialty flavors like basil, citrus, and chilli. The shop also sells seasonings, both not-so-exotic choices like rosemary and sea salt and rarities like Provencal fig vinegar and tomato sablon, intensely flavored tomato powder in sachet pouches. The highlights, though, are the gourmet spreads, especially the olive tapenades combined with the likes of almonds or artichokes, zingy on house-brand crackers like the cookie-textured, chive and oil-enhanced wheat ciappe or the white wine and olive-infused taralli rings. A small selection of cruets, ramekins, and serving bowls, and a few cosmetics like olive soaps, hand creams, and lotions, round out the edibles. Oddly enough, there's nary a fresh olive in sight, although anchovy and red pepper-stuffed varieties are available in jars.

Kathleen Squires NEW YORK SHOPPING

Verdier is the taster for the French olive oil specialists Oliviers & Co., with two shops in Paris and one in Saint Tropez. He not only selected the 15 oils from six countries currently displayed on the shelves in slim glass bottles or beautifully labelled tins, but tastes them every 10 days to be sure they are at their peak of flavour. If one shows signs of fading, he has it removed from the shelves. He can't afford the slightest mistake: at nearly $17 a half-litre, O&CO.'s most expensive oils cost as much as some fine Bordeaux wines. It has been a staple in the Mediterranean diet since ancient times, but the art of tasting it is new.

Because southern France produces much less oil than other traditional olive-producing countries such as Spain and Italy, O&CO. selects oils from all over the Mediterranean. But one of its missions is to revitalize French oil production, nearly wiped out after a devastating freeze in 1956, to produce fruit worthy of good olive oil, and today some French olive oils made with the greatest care by hand-selecting the olives and pressing them within hours in spotlessly clean conditions are challenging the best of

Tuscany and Sicily. Southern France offers an ideal setting for olive trees, which thrive in hot, dry weather at an altitude of around 300 metres.

The northern half of France used to look down on the southern diet of olive oil, garlic and gutsy vegetables such as aubergine and tomato, thinking butter and cream more refined. But that changed as one study after another, starting in the 1940s, showed olive oil's health benefits: it aids digestion, thins the blood (which helps combat heart disease) and builds bone mass. People who adopted olive oil for these qualities grew attached to its flavour. Today, some of the top chefs in Paris – Alain Passard of L'Arpège, William LeDeuil of Les Bookinistes, and Guy Savoy among them – rely on olive oil for their inventive dishes.

The French Paradox
(http://www.frenchhedonist.com/uk/discover/taster.htm)

The shoppers are kings and queens, and more than ever before these kings and queens exercise their power deciding the fate of brands and companies. The *Economist* reports that over 80 per cent of Ford car shoppers in the United States have already researched their purchase on the internet before they arrive at the dealership, armed with a specification sheet showing the precise car they want together with the price they are willing to pay (*Economist*, 2005). But not only car shopping is undergoing radical change. Travel, insurance, music, groceries, consumer electronics and medicine are experiencing a restructuring of shopping patterns. More than anything else the internet has produced this shift of power, and as an agent of change it continuously strengthens the ability of the shopper to set the agenda in the retail environment, redefining not only how we shop, but also the very functionality of a store itself. When shoppers need something they just get it when they want, from where they want and often at the price they want, leaving brands to do nothing but deliver their goods and services while praying that they can meet expectations and price.

However, there still is one other trick left up brands' sleeves – creating wants. As consumers we have reinvented ourselves as shoppers. We have re-imagined the boring chore of buying things we think we need into something fun and exciting. Given the little leisure time we have left, this simply became a necessary and obvious thing to do: turn the boring into exciting. Shoppers have come to expect shopping to be fun, inspiring, fulfilling and convenient – even when grocery shopping. If you do not understand that as a brand or a retailer, you are not catering to their most fundamental shopping desires.

You are not respecting their need for meaningful leisure time. And if you are not up for it, there is a whole world of entertainment, culture, amusement parks, travel, restaurants and so on waiting in line ready to get their share of the shoppers' wallets, a world of alternative ways to spend money.

Apple: merging buying with trying

> It opened at 10 am and more than 800 people rushed in. When we walked past it on my way home from dinner there still seemed to be 800 people inside. Some of them had probably spent the entire day there.
> *Retailization: brand survival in the age of retailer power* (2006)

There is another way of creating retail impact, a technique that by no means is very revolutionary or cutting edge. In fact it is probably as old as the supermarket itself. Think about it. Where and when do you find the most activity in a supermarket? What makes shoppers bustle and congregate? Where do you find actual and direct dialogue between the shopper and the supermarket? The answer? When there is a sampling happening. There is nothing like the tasting of a new pizza snack or a demonstration of a new carpet cleaner to make shoppers stop and get involved. Shoppers love to try stuff out, it is in the very nature of shopping. We try more than we buy, and experienced sales people will tell you that shoppers who sampled the pizza snack or participated in the demonstration of the carpet cleaner will be more likely to buy the product than people who did not. In reality, what we are doing here is merging the second moment of truth (try) into the first (buy) and making them one uniform experience, an experience that is often a very effective way of involving and activating shoppers. What is probably cutting-edge thinking about this is the fact that we very much take it for granted in some categories, but never think about the fact that it is completely absent in most. Would you ever buy a car without having taken it for a spin? How about a pair of jeans? Would you get them without having tried them on for fit and looks? But how come you do not get to try out your new house for a month before making probably the single biggest investment of your life? Or even get a sense of what it is like being at that resort in the Maldives before spending a fortune sending yourself and your family there on an important and much-needed vacation?

A couple of years ago we were on North Michigan Avenue in Chicago. We had gone to see the new Sony Style Centre, which apparently was a new effort by the company to represent itself in retail. Suddenly, we noticed a large white apple on the side of the building next door. We were intrigued and ventured forth. Much to our surprise, this turned out to be one of the new Apple Computer stores. We entered and were greeted by probably the best brand experience we had ever received. The store was simply a pure personification of the joy and genius of the Apple proposition: think different! It opened at 10 am and more than 800 people rushed in. When we walked past it on our way home from dinner there still seemed to be 800 people inside. Some of them had probably spent the entire day there.

Why were they there? They were there for the friendly workstations which allowed them to learn video editing, music production and photo processing. They were there for the Genius Bar, a simple customer-friendly resource that answered all their questions. They were there for the auditorium where they could spend all day learning about Apple products and applications from professional tutors. They were there because they wanted to engage with Apple's innovative and imaginative products. In the process they lived and breathed the Apple brand.

We don't care if Apple sold nothing at their stores – which is patently not the result judging by the lengthy day-long queues in the stores – queues where people seemed genuinely happy to wait. The store was the best brand communications we had ever seen – brand communications that a mere advert could never match, and shopper involvement taken to new, unprecedented levels (Table 12.13).

Next door at the Sony Style Centre, silence echoed around an almost empty store. Now it's closed down! We had seen the future. Apple did not need to sell just one product. It sold the whole company in this involving and inspiring shopping environment. Here was retailization thinking laid out before us in a truly splendid way. Apple has fully realized the retail potential of its brand and fully retailized itself.

Yes, we talk about Apple a lot. But these days, it is a great retail company. We forget that only a few years ago it had no retail presence whatsoever, when Comp USA delisted them from their last US distribution channel. They had a choice. Do a Dell and go onto the internet in a big way or come up with some-

Table 12.13   Apple

APPLE	comments	score (%)
REthink	reinvented the retail concept	99
REimagine	extremely imaginative	99
REstructure	excellent communications and logistics	99
RETAILIZATION	**total involvement**	99

thing entirely different. Being Apple, they chose to be different. It really and truly gets the shopper. Take for instance Apple's Genius Bar, which offers hands-on, real-time advice and tutorials on any given Mac product. Every Apple customer or even every potential Apple customer can schedule same-day time at the Genius Bar, getting a one-on-one dialogue with an Apple representative who can help customers get the most out of their Apple products at no charge. Buying electronics, software and computers is complex, and shoppers are often insecure. What a great way of making the shopper more comfortable by empowering them and involving them in your products. What a great idea and how rarely do we see such shopper-friendly features in the retail environment. Imagine Motorola actually taking the time to teach people how to use its phones. Or imagine Filofax giving people in-store tutorials on how to be better time and task managers. Or imagine that Volvo took the time to make people safer drivers.

The launch of U2's album *How to Dismantle an Atomic Bomb* is a case of integrating media, trends and complementary products. Apple created a special black U2 iPod and the possibility of buying their complete works on iTunes, including previously unreleased work. And they backed this up by giving 'stop the traffic' concerts in New York. The result was significant attention, significant word-of-mouth publicity, record sales and a number one selling disc for U2.

We've been great at creating branded illusions – now we need to get back to shopping realities. Rethink the way we communicate. Now this doesn't mean that advertising doesn't work – it means that we're doing not doing it right!

We need to start pointing in the right direction... towards the points of action... the moments of truth. And it should start with real investments that generate real shopping impact. And give us shoppers who are obsessed about our products... fans. Fans who are really excited about our offerings. The sort of fans like the ones who turned up in their thousands for the opening of the Apple store in Tokyo – the sort of fans that it took a film crew three hours to walk along and film! The sort of fans who beg for your product.

Successful retailization companies like Apple go out of their way to understand their shoppers. They train all their store employees in how to identify market opportunities and target customers... how to know their customers inside out. They argue that you must have a clear idea of how and why your store will be successful. Who will your customers be? Why will they buy from you and not someone else? What products and services will you offer? What people will you need to help you achieve your goals?

The best Apple Centres have a clear understanding of their target segments and customers. Instead of trying to serve every possible customer, they focus their limited time and resources on key segments. This allows them to deliver an exceptional customer experience in a profitable manner. By way of example, consider two imaginary Apple Centres. The first is located in a prime, high-street location. The second is located near an out-of-town business park, not far from a university. It makes little sense for the first Apple Centre to target educational users as their main focus, just as it makes little sense for the second Apple Centre to target home users. This is not an encouragement to ignore customers who don't fit into your target market segments. This is about proactively choosing your target customers (shoppers) at an early stage, rather than waiting to see who eventually visits your Apple Centre. This will allow you to build a profitable, customer-focused business. The best customers are the ones that bring the most reward for your efforts. Choosing your target market segments is therefore simply a matter of economics: which segments can you serve most profitably?

Build your business on the failures of someone else

It's very easy to avoid competing against the leaders – the sectors and brands that can seem to do no wrong. But even they have their failures and sometimes it's an idea to build on them. The iPod by Apple is a good example of what we mean. The iPod was basically a new entry into an established category of moveable music players, dominated by the likes of Sony and Philips. Along comes Apple who redirected the focus of the market and achieved 70 per cent market share in the space of two years. They realized the big boys were not even delivering the next generation of music players and the new MP3 entrants were making little inroads. The rising illegality of music downloads from companies like Napster had made the concept of this market extremely unattractive – despite the fact that this was clearly a new next-generation technology. The record companies were not helping matters as they continued to bury their heads in the sand by sticking to their physical products. Apple decided to reinvent the market by making a product that could keep your entire record collection on one small device. The word spread fast as consumers rushed to convert their collections to this new experience. The catalyst for exponential growth was the iTunes software that made everything so easy.

easyJet: creating choice where there's no choice

easyJet's mission statement is very clear and very transferable... 'to provide its customers with safe, good value, point-to-point air services'.

easyjet.com

We tend to forget that we go out there to steal choice, to steal money from someone else. Understanding the nature of choice is fundamental to understanding who we're competing against. Do you really understand who you're competing against? Have you defined your arena in a limited sense or too wide a sense? Do you really know what shelf you should be operating on? Are you in a category where you represent a priority purchase? Who is creating sales in your arena and how can you steal that sale? Or should we be fighting in a new arena?

Sometimes our competition forgets how to compete. Sometimes they think the way forward is to eliminate choice. Big mistake! When there's no choice – give them a choice. We recently met an old man of 75-odd years travelling to Stockholm on a Ryanair flight from London. He asked us whether we knew any hostels he could sleep at. Why was a 75-year-old man travelling like this? After a discussion it emerged that Ryanair had changed his life. He could now afford to travel somewhere he'd never been every two weeks – the first time in his life such an opportunity had been open to him. He grasped that opportunity with both hands. Budget airlines represent one of the biggest breakthrough businesses of recent years. Southwest Airlines in the United States is often cited as the definitive case study in this area. However, the more interesting and relevant case studies are within the European airline market.

easyJet is a company that understood from the early days that all, and they mean all, markets are vulnerable to competition. The European airline market had spent many years as a 'cosy cartel' where national carriers could control their hub at the expense of competition and consumer choice. They had exclusive rights – rights they would not give up. They had to a large extent eliminated choice. It was time to give it back.

Then along came easyJet (and initially Ryanair), which effectively side-stepped the whole stagnant market. They fully understood the competition and decided to go around it. They created their own hubs – provincial airports close to major cities that in most cases were barely surviving. The provincial airports welcomed this invasion of new business opportunities and in many cases paid these new airlines to come and use their resources. Thus the expensive landing fees were effectively eliminated. To reduce costs further they introduced a new no-frills operation with planes utilized to their maximum capacity. The planes, incidentally, were the newest fleet in Europe – not your traditional perspective on a budget airline. Most bookings were internet based and interchangeable. The big national carriers would often charge you up to 10 times more and allow no changes!

As one of the pioneers in the low-cost airline market, easyJet base their business on a number of principles:

- Minimize distribution costs by using the internet to take bookings. About 90 per cent of all easyJet tickets are sold via the web. This makes the company one of Europe's largest internet retailers.
- Maximize efficient use of their assets, by decreasing turnaround time at airports.
- A 'simple-service model' means the end of free on-board catering.
- Ticketless travel, where passengers receive an e-mail confirming their booking, cuts the cost of issuing, distributing and processing tickets.
- Intensive use of IT in their administration and management, aiming to run a paperless office.

They in essence created a whole new way of retailizing their product offering. They have transformed the European market to the extent that Ryanair has become the largest passenger carrier in Europe and alone made more money than the top three national carriers in 2005 (BA, AF and KLM) did in total. easyJet carried more than 20 million passengers last year.

easyJet's mission statement is very clear and very transferable:

- to provide its customers with safe, good value, point-to-point air services;
- to effect and to offer a consistent and reliable product and fares appealing to leisure and business markets on a range of European routes.

To achieve this they will develop their people and establish lasting relationships with their suppliers.

In the case of easyJet they have taken this philosophy one step further and are now actively investing in easyCar, easyInternetcafe, easyCruise, easyCinema and easyPhone.

Wherever the competition is entrenched and complacent they offer a price/service model that transforms the way you buy the product – from easycarRental with one-hour rentals to easyPhone where you buy cheap capacity. If you look more closely at one of these new businesses, they have clearly learnt lessons from their easyJet business. easyInternetcafe's mission statement is 'to be the world's leading Internet café chain that is the cheapest way to get online'.

Their principles build from their experience to date:

- We will achieve the lowest cost base among our competitors – home and mobile access and other Internet cafés – by keeping the business simple.
- We will offer 'no-frills' access to the world wide web, while maintaining content filtering to avoid causing offence.
- We will use commodity equipment wherever possible. We have, however, developed and use our proprietary automated billing system

and vending machines, enabling unattended operations hence
reducing labour costs.

- Our billing system allows us to use yield management techniques to
  maximize utilization and revenue from our assets.
- Our points of presence ('POPs') will be co-located within the premises
  of other businesses ('Hosts') to minimize our exposure to non-core
  'shopkeeping' activities.
- We will develop a strong people culture and align the interests of our
  staff with those of our shareholders in order to create a profitable
  business and long-term value.

Is there any business they couldn't transform with these principles? They
have shown that you don't always have to attack entrenched competitors
(Table 12.14). You do, however, have to offer a choice or, even better, a
new choice.

Table 12.14   easyJet

easyJet	Comments	Score (%)
REthink	a genuine pioneer	80
REimagine	consistently inventive	80
REstructure	has to be good	70
RETAILIZATION	**creating choice where there's no choice**	77

Red Bull: rewriting the rules

'Don't quit your day job!' The market research results were devastating. The thin color of the new drink was totally unappetizing, the
sticky mouth feel and taste were deemed 'disgusting'. And the
concept of 'stimulates mind and body' was rated irrelevant. The
verdict by the research firm: 'No other new product has ever failed
this convincingly.'

Alex Wipperfürth from *Brand Hijack*

It's worth noting that incremental innovation is not the only way. It doesn't
have to be about incremental development. There are companies that have
looked hard and long at the competition and decided it isn't about incremental change – it's about a completely 'new' competition in a completely
unexpected fashion. They not only understood the context – they often

changed the context. They even changed the available choice and in some cases brought consumers to a market they never really dreamed they would be in. They look at the competition and say there's a new, much better way of doing this. Sometimes even a better way of communicating our winning strengths. 'No other new product has ever failed this convincingly' was the result of a research test on a new energy-giving beverage. That beverage, Red Bull, has gone on to be one of the most successful soft drink launches of recent years and is now a five billion dollar business. It beat the odds by throwing conventional marketing wisdom overboard. It understood the limitations of its own product and the competition and developed a powerful new go-to-market process. It established a new category – the legal, yet hip stimulant – and it ignored the issue of taste and sold the product at a price point eight times higher than Coke. It did all this by **rewriting the rules**.

It used communications to develop a cult following for the brand over a period of five years. It also understood that context was everything and used the context as its shelf. Wherever people are tired and staying up all night, or otherwise in search of a pick-me up, became the context and the driving force behind all the company's marketing efforts, from product sampling to sponsoring and hosting events. The often misperceived thing about Red Bull is that it chases cool. What it really does, however, is chase anyone who needs an energy boost. It became cool because of the way it was marketed – not to whom it was marketed.

Red Bull is an example of a brand that finally tipped, when the market created new uses and rituals. 'It became a mainstream staple as soon as bartenders introduced the Stoli Bully across Europe. The legendary cocktail, comprised of Red Bull and Vodka, was rumored to have the power of ecstasy. Red Bull's sales force could have never dictated a signature drink to bartenders. But by targeting on-premise distribution at trendy night spots, they were able to facilitate the product usage evolution of its brand by its early market' (Alex Wipperfürth from *Brand Hijack*).

Alex Wipperfürth in his excellent book took a closer look at some of the fundamental differences; at how Red Bull consistently and successfully manages to do the opposite of what everybody else does; how they rewrote the rules:

- Positioning
    - Conventional mindset: Create a socially aspiring image
    - Red Bull mindset: Create a functional foundation: show how the drink fits into people's way of life
- Advertising
    - Conventional mindset: Advertising launches the brand and stays the lead marketing tool

- Red Bull mindset: Advertising airs only after the launch phase and plays a limited and specific role within the marketing mix
- Targeting
  - Conventional mindset: All consumers are created equal.
  - Red Bull mindset: Some consumers are definitely more equal than others.
- Distribution
  - Conventional mindset: Broad availability is used to create demand.
  - Red Bull mindset: Create demand before broadening availability.
- Marketing mix (sampling)
  - Conventional mindset: Sampling is all about quantity (reach).
  - Red Bull mindset: Sampling is all about quality (much lower reach, yet the experience of a tangible difference).
- Celebrity sponsorship
  - Conventional mindset: Celebrity endorsement has a steep price, but gets publicity.
  - Red Bull mindset: Pursue those celebrities who are fans of Red Bull, but don't pay them.
- Merchandising
  - Conventional mindset: Keep merchandising in consumer reach.
  - Red Bull mindset: Keep merchandising out of consumer reach.
- Network relationships
  - Conventional mindset: Vendors are lucky to work for us!
  - Red Bull mindset: Treat all stakeholders as partners.
- Corporate leadership
  - Conventional mindset: Clear annual volume and profit objectives and fast financial payout.
  - Red Bull mindset: Patience and investment.

Of course, the big boys wanted to copy this success, but have so far met with limited success. They lack the spirit and patience of the Red Bull approach – and the communications, let alone the rules (Table 12.15).

Table 12.15   Red Bull

Red Bull	comments	score (%)
REthink	turned an 'impossible' product into a success	80
REimagine	created their own very original mindset	85
REstructure	use mindset to the extreme	85
RETAILIZATION	**rewriting the rules**	83

Procter & Gamble: the moments of truth

Buying – the first moment of truth

P&G, the world's biggest brand company, has been dealing with the future for quite a while. As A G Lafley, the head of P&G, succinctly stated, it's all about the moments of truth and to him there are only two moments of truth: buying and trying. There are only two moments of truth, when people buy your product and when people try your product.

The 'first moment of truth', as P&G calls it, is the three to seven seconds when someone notices an item on a store shelf, when shoppers are about to buy the product. Despite spending billions on traditional advertising, the consumer-products giant thinks this instant is one of its most important marketing opportunities. It created a position 18 months ago, Director of First Moment of Truth, or Director of FMOT (pronounced 'EFF-mott'), to produce sharper, flashier in-store displays. There's a 15-person FMOT department at P&G headquarters in Cincinnati as well as 50 FMOT leaders stationed around the world (*WSJ*, 2005).

At Procter & Gamble, Dina Howell, the director of FMOT, says she wants to take in-store marketing 'from an art to a science'. P&G has developed a series of tests to measure the success of its packaging and in-store marketing efforts. P&G won't divulge specific details. But broadly speaking, Ms Howell says packaging should 'interrupt' shoppers on their shopping trip. P&G has developed a set of questions that a brand must answer:

- Who am I?
- What am I?
- Why am I right for you?

P&G has had a genuine insight. It has realized that the old adage of above the line is strategic and below the line is tactical no longer holds. In fact it is totally reversed. Above the line is now increasingly tactical and below the line is increasingly strategic.

P&G's insight is helping to power a shift in the advertising business: the growing sophistication of in-store marketing. Almost a century ago, P&G popularized the concept of mass-market advertising. Now, in response to the fragmentation of television and print ads, it wants to tout its brands directly to consumers where they're most likely to be influenced: in the store.

One of P&G's most important beliefs is 'the consumer is boss', and that it is always profitable to listen carefully to the boss. Today maybe they should be saying 'the shopper is boss'.

When ad agencies submit ideas, P&G invites them to two facilities it built several years ago in Cincinnati and Geneva. These mock stores double as research centres where P&G can rearrange shelves and see how its products look alongside those of the competition. The company also brings in focus-group participants to study how they shop.

For the launch of Kandoo wipes – flushable baby wipes for toilet-training toddlers – in the United States, P&G convinced retailers to place the packages low on shelves, so they would be at a toddler's eye-level. It also created display shelves in the shape of the product's frog mascot to attract children's attention.

Jim Stengel, global marketing officer for P&G, is one of the advertising industry's harshest critics, awarding it a 'C minus' for its ability to embrace new media. P&G recently launched a major global review of its 60 million dollar point-of-sale budgets and Larry Light, who has been giving McDonald's a makeover as its chief marketing officer, says bluntly: 'The days of mass marketing are over'. To keep in touch with their customers, consumer-goods companies are shifting their spending away from traditional media, such as network TV and print, to other types of promotion.

A decade ago, P&G used to put about 90 per cent of its advertising budget into TV, but now it spreads the money more widely. For some new products, TV may account for only a quarter of total spending. Within P&G's $4 billion advertising budget, a growing proportion is shifting from mainstream media, such as television, radio and print, to new media and other forms of sales promotion, such as direct mail, public relations, promotions, sponsorship and product placement. Collectively this sort of spending, sometimes called 'below-the-line' advertising, or marketing services, is already worth more than twice what is spent on traditional display advertising. Together, the two sorts of spending added up to more than $1 trillion last year, says WPP, a leading advertising group. Brands are increasingly refocusing on the real future – the retail future.

In part for this reason, the decades-old hierarchy that ruled the ad industry is under assault. Previously, ad executives who designed TV commercials looked down on those who worked on in-store promotions. Now, executives with retail expertise are gaining clout as the world's biggest advertising firms build up departments to handle an area in which they have little expertise. One marketing firm has even hired an expert on the durability of corrugated cardboard.

To fill a store's giant canvas with advertising messages, ad agencies are now charged with designing everything from in-store TV commercials to special shelf displays and packaging. The work is more elaborate than traditional in-store marketing, typically signs posted at the end of super-market aisles. For all the excitement, agencies face huge challenges co-ordinating so many pieces. Some are stumbling over new problems, such as how to measure and charge for these services. To market Pampers diapers in the United Kingdom, P&G persuaded retailers to put fake doorknobs high up on restroom doors, to remind parents how much babies need to stretch.

P&G, the maker of Tide, Crest and Pampers, won't say how much it spends on in-store marketing. But it has cut its commitments to advertise on cable channels for the current season by 25 per cent and its broadcast-TV allotment is down about 5 per cent. At the same time, overall ad spending rose slightly.

Trying – the second moment of truth

Then there's the second moment of truth – trying. As we described earlier, tryvertising is a new way of thinking about mass communications – a new way of getting trial. It's about encouraging loyalty from day one by providing potential shoppers with a real product experience. Coined by trendwatching.com, tryvertising is all about consumers getting familiar with new products by actually trying them out. Think of tryvertising as a new, exciting type of product placement. It's not about free shampoo samples in magazines, or a point-of-sale promotion stand in a supermarket. It's about the real world and integrating your goods and services into daily life in a relevant way, so that consumers can make up their mind based on their experience, not your messages. So what does tryvertising include? Think 'obvious' activities like handing out product samples, and more subtle, inte-grated product placements that are part of an experience or solution. It's everything from new-style sachets containing single servings of liquid products, to hotels partnering with luxury carmakers to offer high-end model test drives to guests during their stay. The main communication chal-lenge here has been ensuring relevance and guaranteeing that products are tried out at the right time, in the right spot, and by the right target audience.

P&G has already started down this path with its Tremor project, where it has formed a community of teens. Tremor is a marketing service – powered by the Procter & Gamble Company – that develops teen word-of-mouth marketing programmes by recruiting teens to help develop exciting and relevant product ideas and marketing programmes that teens want to talk about.

Tremor works with companies in industries like entertainment, fashion, music, food and beauty. Their members are directly involved in the creation and launch of these companies' ideas and programmes to build word-of-mouth among teenagers. In only two years this focus group cum sample/coupon dispersing network signed up 280,000 US teens, ages 13 to 19, who actively promote new products to their peers, and may be asked to place coupons and product samples in living rooms, schools and any other relevant locations.

Innovation, innovation, innovation...

The most successful grower of brands in the mass markets is arguably P&G. P&G has built the biggest brand business in the world by understanding its competition and understanding the context the competition plays within. Their key to growth has been continuous improvements to their brand fighters through a constant series of innovations which add small additional fighting features to their armoury. Segmentation and line extensions have been their game as they have constantly sought to win their arena. Their innovations have come from understanding their competitors and finding ways to beat them.

Incremental change is the name of the game. Staying one step ahead is their yardstick of measurement. And a very successful strategy it has been. P&G has over 16 brands exceeding sales of 1 billion dollars each and is the global leader in four core product categories: fabric and home care, beauty care, baby and family care, and health care. Only in snacks and beverages do they fail to dominate their competitors. They have the keys to their categories – their shelf space.

Organizing your product development

> Our vision is simple. We want P&G to be known as the company that collaborates – inside and out – better than any other company in the world
> A G Lafley, CEO, P&G

We need to find more new product solutions for a new future. They increasingly need to be 'out of the box' and retail-centric solutions. In the 21st century, innovation involves trying to deal with an extended and rapidly advancing scientific frontier, fragmenting markets, political uncertainties, regulatory instabilities and competitors who are increasingly coming from unexpected directions. The response has to be one of spreading the net wide and trying to make use of a broad range of knowledge signals. In other words, learning to manage innovation at a network level. Even the largest and most established innovators are recognizing this shift. Sometimes the most conservative companies are coming up with the most radical solutions to help them find new product solutions. They recognize that finding great new ideas requires thinking from everywhere. A good example of this can be found at Procter & Gamble, which launched its dedicated Connect + Develop programme about five years ago, with the goal of having at least 50 per cent of its new products derived from ideas generated by non-employee outside experts.

They spend about 2 billion dollars a year on this activity and they have set themselves the ambitious goal of sourcing much of their idea input from outside the company. Beside its own R&D employee base of 7,000, the company now has access to millions of potential innovators. The results so far? Everything from Swiffer Wet Jet, Olay Daily Facials, Crest, Whitestrips & Night Effects to Mr. Clean Autodry, Kandoo baby wipes and Lipfinity (source: Tech Central Station, *Industry Week*). In the past five years, the annual study published by Information Resources, Inc. has consistently ranked P&G products among the top 10 new brands and line extensions in the consumer packaged goods industry. Similar stories can be heard at other companies, including IBM, Cisco and Intel.

P&G has got it right. Pretty well all of it, through an insightful leveraging of the key moments of truth (Table 12.16).

Table 12.16 P&G

P&G	comments	score (%)
REthink	the two moments of truth lead the way	95
REimagine	constantly innovate	95
REstructure	increasingly effective	95
RETAILIZATION	**the moments of truth**	95

Gillette: constant innovation

Other big brand builders like Gillette have followed the same pattern for years. They, like P&G, understand that product innovation must be constant with noticeable or at least marketable improvements year in year out – which is probably just as well now that P&G own them. In today's market a company can't count on consumer loyalty and instead must constantly 'sell' the customer on product value. Sensor, launched in 1990, was the first major new product introduction for Gillette for 25 years. When BIC disposables threatened to turn the market into a cheap commodity one, Gillette responded with Sensor – a new shaving experience (or apparently new). There was only one blade then and one lubrastrip. But step by step blades and lubrastrips and more and more floating heads were added to produce the ultimate shave in perception terms; innovation after innovation from Mach 1 to Mach 3, the new battery-powered system. But did you know (and one of us was there) that Mach 3 was on the drawing table in 1990 – sometimes there's a time and a place to be new and innovative. It waited 15 years for its market entry.

The incremental innovations from Gillette have kept the brand securely positioned as the global leader. It still maintains a 70+ per cent global market share, a uniquely remarkable performance for such a high-consumption product. It's understood its competition from the beginning and has always kept one step ahead (Table 12.17).

P&G and Gillette arguably have four rules for success:

1. Consumers will pay a premium for products that offer improvements over either private label or the brands they have bought for years. By fully understanding your competition you will understand where those improvements need to be. Innovation for the sake of innovation is a pointless exercise.
2. Improvements over your competition must be constant with noticeable (or at least marketable) improvements year in year out. You're in for the long haul.
3. Improvements must be designed to 'upscale' consumer preferences. Selling clean and cavity-free teeth isn't as profitable as selling whiter teeth. Selling coffee isn't as profitable as selling Cappucino experiences.
4. The upscaling of tastes applies to every rung of the consumer hierarchy, not just the affluent. A budget airline is upscale to someone who previously couldn't afford to fly. This tried and tested formula has stood the test of time.

Is it more important to think out of the box than inside the box? Is Gillette so invulnerable? Could someone produce a product that shaves better? Why not! – all we're doing is cutting. To date, blades have done a great job. Tomorrow, controllable laser beams or sonic destroyers or genetically engineered creams that keep you stubble-free for weeks. If we can produce supercomputers, surely we can get a smoother shave! We wait to see.

Table 12.17 Gillette

GILLETTE	Comments	Score (%)
REthink	always trying to stay ahead	85
REimagine	continuous innovation	85
REstructure	efficient	85
RETAILIZATION	**constant innovation**	85

ASSA ABLOY: solve a problem

> The development of this new concept and the opening of the store are the result of extensive research done in Australia, France, Germany, UK and Scandinavia. The aim was to identify the needs and problems that consumers face with regard to locks and other products developed to increase the safety and security of their homes.
>
> Åke Sund, Executive Group Vice President,
> Market and Business Development

As we discussed earlier, we live in a world of the probably unstoppable global retailers. They have grown constantly, developed their abilities and successfully understood their environments. They have improved execution in-store due to better understanding of the shopper and serviced them with increasingly better value propositions. But that hunt for value is at a cost – squeezed and struggling brands (critical eye.com).

Stop, you say – it couldn't happen to me. Well, it could. Those same forces we described early on are starting to affect all industries. Take ASSA ABLOY, the Stockholm-headquartered multibillion dollar company that represents the biggest locking solutions company in the world, with over 100 leading brands in over 125 countries. This is a company that traditionally hasn't needed to worry about retailers of any size. It has been essentially a business-to-business company supplying local professional distributors. But their world is now undergoing radical change:

- They are increasingly trying to reach the consumer directly to grow their business. This has put them increasingly in conversations with the big mass retailers of the world.
- They are having to deal with giant DIY retailers like B&Q which has now become a European and beyond super-retailer.
- They are actively embracing category management as a key operational discipline.
- They are actively training their staff worldwide on the importance of retail to the growth of their business.
- They are developing a retail concept for their existing and new partners.

From B2B to B2C

The last one is maybe the most dynamic one. The most effective way of making sure nothing stands between you and your shopper is to create your own arena! Become a retailer. Create your own proprietary distribution.

ASSA ABLOY have for a long time realized they need their own presence in the high street to better promote their ideas and brands. In order to completely understand the consumers locking needs, ASSA ABLOY needed to be face to face with their shoppers. There was a need for a channel that solely focused on the consumer and where they were able to spend the time needed to win the shoppers' confidence.

ASSA ABLOY recently undertook a major problem detection study (PDS) with consumers around the world. This technique was originally developed by BBDO Worldwide 30 years ago and has long been a mainstay technique for assessing positioning development. It's a very effective way to understand the limitations and opportunities of the categories you operate in. Federal Express used this technique a number of years ago to better understand how they could improve their product offering. They simply asked consumers what the perceived problems with their delivery service were. The answer was clear: they did not like the loss of control from delivering their product to a Fedex office to the recipient receiving it. The gap was one big black hole, a hole on which they had no information. Fedex developed an online monitoring system called Fedex Track which could show their customers exactly where their parcel was at any point of time. The result: a happy customer who could let his or her recipient know what was going on at any point of time – and a clear competitive advantage.

PDS can even be used to identify a market opportunity where none seemed to exist, which is exactly how ASSA ABLOY used it. They wanted to know how consumers viewed the installation of locks and security systems. The feedback was overwhelming; consumers everywhere were incredibly dissatisfied with the present forms of distribution. They complained about lack of control, lack of information and non-existent back-up services within the traditional locksmith and DIY distribution channels. As a result, ASSA ABLOY has developed its own proprietary distribution channel called Yale Security Point, designed to give customers the sort of service quality they desperately wanted. The stores are designed to be a one-stop shop for extensive home security products and service offerings. Home owners visiting the unique new style of showroom could view and discuss security options and arrange for customized locking solutions to be installed in their homes. The focus is entirely on the residential market. Yale's present distribution partners servicing the residential market segment are invited to cooperate.

Yale Security Point is a 'Do It For Me' concept. It first provides the customer with information about home security and then offers a complete customized solution, starting with a security evaluation and carrying it through to a completed installation. Yale Security Point trained consultants to visit customers' homes, provide an assessment to identify any security weak spots, and analyse customers' needs to design affordable, tailor-made locking solutions. The stores showcase premium products that provide increased convenience, security and safety features while meeting local standards. The store allows people to experience first-hand the most exciting new products and the latest advances in residential security technology. Stores have already opened in the UK, Germany and South Africa. More are planned worldwide.

In one simple move ASSA ABLOY, which is almost exclusively a business-to-business corporation, has added a significant business bringing a consumer revenue stream to its overall efforts. In effect, it has realized the very essence of its business needs to evolve from B2B to B2C (Table 12.18). The key to that evolution is retail.

The most important point here is that literally anyone can build a strong retail presence. If an industrial lock company can do it, anyone can. Even you.

From B2C to B2B2S

The other thing that Yale has realized in its dealings with retailers is that we are no longer in the simple era of business-to-consumer shopping. We have to move beyond B2C. We are no longer even selling to the consumer. We are selling to a more difficult and less understood customer – the shopper – as well as to a more discerning business customer – the retailer and particularly the global retailer. B2C becomes B2B2S (business to business retailer to shopper). This change in focus requires a whole new way of thinking.

At one extreme we need to start understanding our shoppers. Forget consumers and embrace shoppers. This is an age that has produced a world where we increasingly live and consummate our whole being from satisfaction to entertainment in one place – the shop. Shopping is where it happens! Shopping is the place where the two new powers of our society converge: the shopper kings and queens and the retail emperors. Shopping is a world that demands efficient connections between brands,

Table 12.18 ASSA ABLOY

ASSA ABLOY	Comments	Score (%)
REthink	had insights into shopper need	80
REimagine	still evolving	80
REstructure	needs investment	70
RETAILIZATION	solve a problem	76

retailers and shoppers. Do everything you can to understand your shopper and make those connections work smoothly. At the other extreme you need new relationships with your present big retail customers. As a traditional B2B company, Yale has always been used to dealing with multiple retail customers and has developed considerable expertise in developing productive proactive relationships with them. Today, most of the B2C markets are relationships based on conflict and 'us and them' philosophies. Stop fighting (or surrendering) and start cooperating. The more enlightened retailers and brands realize that the most successful future will be created through cooperation or co-opetition. The benefits of cooperation between retailer and brands are increased influence, lower risks and better sales. The dangers of non-cooperation are well understood and help no one. To make cooperation a reality, brands must start to think of retail proactively and as an important investment priority with a quantifiable return.

Retail has become an issue that all brand corporations need to embrace globally – an issue they have to deal with simply to survive. All these things will lead to a new approach to branding: an approach that leverages the power of retail thinking to your brand and allows you to reconnect to the shopper; an approach that takes us back to one of the core priorities of any business – creating sales. And finally, it's worth remembering that we're all retailers. We're all in the business of selling. Our own raison d'être isn't that different from tomorrow's global retailers. We both seek the same thing: the shopper.

Peroni: challenging perceptions

'We want to challenge people's perception of beer drinking.'

Today's retail battlefield is an intense and increasingly competitive battleground for attention. To achieve success, brands must address five critical consumer issues that can bring the two moments of truth alive – issues that can ensure you produce the best selling situations possible:

- They must instil trust with your consumer.
- They must prove beyond reasonable doubt that they are better than the competition.
- They must reassure shoppers that they offer genuine value.
- They must make shoppers comfortable and at ease about their purchase decision.
- They must set the correct tone and manner for the brand–customer relationship in order for future loyalty to be maintained and reinforced.

To meet these purchase challenges, brands must offer a profitable and enduring branded value proposition. They must also create a differentiated and relevant purchase experience and fully deliver on their pre-purchase promise. It is critical that they make an unforgettable impact that plants the seed for a long-term relationship and make it easy for shoppers to commit, now and in the future.

All of the above has become an increasingly complicated task – a task that requires and demands new thinking. You think of the great brands and you think of TV ads – but were they really the key to success? Did Coke, Nike, P&G and Timberland see retail communications as the key? From Nike with its Nike city super-outlets to Timberland's uniquely designed shop environments to the sustained retail promotional initiatives of P&G and Coca Cola – these are brands that actively embrace RETAILIZATION today.

Those new ways can sometimes take your breath away. The brewery Peroni has rented a store on Sloane Street (one of the most expensive areas in London) and painted it all white inside. The only thing in the store is a bottle of Peroni on a pedestal standing in the middle of the store. And a fridge (all white, of course). Peroni has taken the minimalistic thoughts from fashion (Gucci, Prada, etc) and brought them into the beer industry. This is all done because Peroni is re-launching their beer with a new label and a longer neck (bottle) which reflects the Italian joy of life. 'We want to challenge people's perception of beer-drinking', they claim. Peroni is also starting to sell accessories, bags and clothes. Peroni wants to create a debate on their store. They may well have succeeded (Table 12.19).

Table 12.19   Peroni

PERONI	comments	score (%)
REthink	trying to be different	80
REimagine	imaginative	70
REstructure	OK	60
RETAILIZATION	challenging	70

H&M: four seconds to get them!

Our success depends on what customers think when they meet us, and we believe that our customer spends four seconds to decide whether they like the meeting or not.

H&M CEO Rolf Eriksen

Retailization is not a department, it is a way of thinking that should involve your entire organization. This means you should start getting curious and involving the world around you. It also means that your whole company should live and breathe retailization. It is not something you implement, it is something you earn. You need to get everyone involved in becoming one retail-centric, shopper-loving selling machine.

H&M CEO Rolf Eriksen explains in the book *Retailization*: 'At H&M we've for years compared ourselves to Native American tribes on the prairie hunting for buffalo. The scouts were able to put their ear to the ground and locate the animals and then everybody would join in on the hunt. At H&M we approach our business the same way, we want all our employees to be scouts and hunters. Our stores are the prairie and we solve all our challenges through the store. We solve all customer issues through the store. And we incentivize all our employees to listen carefully to what the shopper wants. We listen and then hunt together for solutions. This is what we're always striving to master.'

H&M, the Swedish retailer, are particularly adroit at creating retail buzz or BUZZR through co-opetition with leading fashion suppliers. Building on the enormous success of their Karl Lagerfield collection, they have taken many further steps. They signed Stella McCartney to follow their collaboration with Karl Lagerfeld, in a deal that saw the designer creating a 40-piece collection for the Scandinavian label. Retail prices for the Stella collection were along the lines of Lagerfeld's immensely successful collection, which caused pandemonium in H&M stores as shoppers fought over $19.90 T-shirts and $149 wool–cashmere coats. Shoppers even flew from Tokyo for the opening! Stella's line for H&M was exclusively women's wear, unlike that by Karl, who also created a variety of men's looks, in particular his signature high-collar dress shirts. The McCartney link-up was an ideal follow-up to the Lagerfeld project, which generated enormous worldwide attention for H&M, burnishing its reputation as a supplier of hip, fashionable clothes at highly affordable prices. A major international advertising campaign, including outdoor and television publicity for the collection by Stella, backed up the idea.

In tapping Stella for this project, the cerebral Scandinavian executives at H&M used a logical approach. They polled shoppers in their vast chain and discovered that Stella was the best-known designer to their clientele. All this has also helped Stella. Apart from sales, her 32 million dollar company benefits from the marketing clout of a seven and a half billion one. Their latest initiative is flamboyant design team Viktor and Rolf, who treated fashionistas to a glimpse of their new capsule collection for H&M in a lavish, wedding-themed spectacular in Beverly Hills to launch the idea in the

United States. The cult Paris-based label by Dutch duo Viktor Horsting and Rolf Snoeren, who are renowned for the modern twist they give to classically tailored clothes, has combined lush satin fabrics with sharp silhouettes in its new lines.

Working with these renowned designers has given fashion 'street cred' to both retailers, as it has allowed regular shoppers the chance to buy what people normally have to spend thousands of dollars to own. And the low prices that customers pay for this trendy gear means that when it goes out of style two weeks later they can feel OK about tossing it to one side and heading right back to H&M for the fresher styles.

Of course, shopping cheap-chic isn't only for those of us who can't afford actual-chic any more. Fans of H&M's styles include Gwen Stefani, Shakira, Kanye West and the Olsen twins. While H&M's paid spokesmodel, Madonna, is a great choice for such a global brand, free endorsements from names like these can do wonders for any retailer, particularly in the US market.

Going global

This is a major priority for H&M. In terms of growth prospects, though, the difference between H&M and other global retailers like Gap is that when Gap says 'global', they mean the United States, Canada, the UK, France and Japan. Since 2003 alone H&M have entered eight new countries, including Ireland and Hungary in 2005. Most remarkable, though, is that as established as the brand is, H&M has fewer than 100 stores in the United States, compared to thousands of stores for Gap, and they are now preparing to enter the Asian market through Shanghai and Hong Kong in 2007 (Motley Fool, 2006).

Keep it fresh

The first rule is short and sweet: keep it fresh. As shoppers, we love fresh things. That's why they place the fruit and vegetable department at the front of the supermarket. It shapes our perception of the store's quality and impacts the overall freshness perception of the entire supermarket.

Freshness stimulates us and awakens our curiosity. Rolf Erikson, H&M CEO, comments: 'Dealing with fashion products is a lot like working with fast-moving consumer goods – both have an expiration date. Every time we work with a new trend we must be able to renew ourselves. Customers today want innovation. We get new products in our stores daily. The challenge lies in innovation; being able to dare being on the cutting edge.' (Table 12.20)

IT ONLY TAKES FOUR SECONDS... and that's on a good day. Some people already know how to deal with this new future, this new era.

Table 12.20   H&M

H&M	comments	score (%)
REthink	making four seconds work	90
REimagine	consistently innovative	90
REstructure	internationally developing	90
RETAILIZATION	**four seconds**	90

To repeat what we said at the beginning from Rolf Eriksen, CEO of H&M: 'Our success depends on what customers think when they meet us, and we believe that our customer spends four seconds to decide whether they like the meeting or not'. Those four seconds are a critical stretch of time. While they're only four seconds, our total commitment should be about making the meeting happen.

Courvoisier: REvitalization

It's not quite the same world.

Anne-Sophie Louvet

Instead of just communicating to your target group, you have to become a part of their reality. You have to become whole-heartedly involved. Subculturizing is a strong and unique way of strengthening your market presence. With the target group itself, as the primary medium and message, you are able to create stronger and greater loyalty. Subculturizing can be a more cost- and result-efficient way of reaching a larger audience. However, you must have an in-depth insight into your target group and also a carefully planned and progressive tactical approach to the use of tools as media devices – and genuine interest and dedication towards your target group. You must be aware that it is a dangerous tactic if it goes wrong and your target group turns away from your product and brand. But the reward is enormous if you succeed!

You can even be part of a subculture and not even be aware of it! The brandy brand Courvoisier has experienced a revitalizing of its brands through the embracement of the hip-hop subculture. For this culture it is the symbol of wealth. MCs as diverse as Common and Snoop have long lauded Cognac as a drink of choice, with more recent references in 2003's hit single

Pass The Courvoisier which featured a video showcasing Busta, Pharrell and P Diddy partying it up in a bar filled with beautiful women and hundreds of gleaming bottles of Courvoisier. Songs like 'Courvoisier' have produced a following among urban youths, who have been known to mix the liquor in new concoctions such as 'Thug Passion' and 'French Connection'. Jay's newly opened 40/40 Club even includes a 'Remy Room' in salute to Remy Martin, his favourite Cognac brand. 'Cognac is a classy, sophisticated and really smooth thing to drink,' Jay-Z told *The Wall Street Journal*.

The Cognac industry is now prospering thanks to nearly tripled Cognac exports to the United States in the past 10 years. Furthermore, Americans spent approximately $1 billion on the French spirit in 2005. Interestingly, Cognac's surging US sales are parallel to hip-hop's mainstream growth. Americans imported 3.7 million cases of Cognac in 2005, 36 per cent of the worldwide market, compared to 1.3 million in 1993. According to *The Wall Street Journal*, Hennessy, America's biggest Cognac brand with 53 per cent of the market, claims that young blacks represent 60–85 per cent of US sales.

Though America's infatuation with Cognac has salvaged its industry, the flip side is that French grape growers responsible for Cognac are dumb-founded upon witnessing rap's use of the brand. 'It's not quite the same world', Anne-Sophie Louvet, a 44-year-old woman who cultivates her great-grandfather's 113-year-old vineyards told *The Wall Street Journal*. 'In this region, you don't show your wealth if you have some, and you don't talk about money,' she added. There are many other examples. Think about American BlackBerry which kick-started the US short message system (SMS) industry. In the United States they talk about BlackBerrying, whereas in Denmark they talk about SMSing. They specifically targeted their effort towards the hip-hop subculture as a carrier of their product and culture – and eventually the worldwide rap trend carried it to the mass market and it literally flew off the shelf (Table 12.21).

Table 12.21 Courvoisier

COURVOISIER	comments	score (%)
REthink	grasped subculture opportunity	85
REimagine	imaginative	80
REstructure	OK	70
RETAILIZATION	**REvitalization**	79

Senseo: brand co-creation

Changing the arena can also sometimes allow you to bring brands back from the dead. Products often launch brands. They also revitalize them and when thought through properly can make a huge difference. Philips, working with Sara Lee, a coffee manufacturer, has managed to bring life to a pretty boring business by creating a new shelf. The two brands have in effect co-opeted with each other and co-created a new idea, an alliance that we think will become a key way forward in the future.

Philips have evolved a highly successful alternative to traditional coffee makers. Electronics giant Philips and global consumer goods manufacturer Sara Lee figured out that in most busy families the big 12-cup, coffee-all-day machine was becoming obsolete. Not to mention the ever-rising millions of people who live alone and don't even know what to do with traditional coffee makers anymore. Throw in a meteoric rise in upscale coffee's popularity, and you have the perfect market for Philips and Sara Lee's 'Senseo', a coffee machine that serves up just one or two tasty, fresh cups of creamy coffee, using sophisticated Senseo coffee 'pads' that come in various flavours. The machine is priced at €69 (roughly US $90), with coffee pads costing roughly €10–15 cents per piece.

In 2005 Senseo coffee machines clearly demonstrated to the world just how creative and involving tryvertising can be by using this new product innovation directly as a way to involve shoppers. Senseo replaced traditional bus-stop billboards with ones that were not so traditional, with built-in coffee machines offering waiting passengers a cup of free freshly brewed coffee (Table 12.22).

Consumers are going for Senseo in a big way. Senseo has sold 800,000 machines in the Netherlands since its introduction in 2001, brewing more than 10 million cups a day and capturing 10 per cent of the entire coffee market. After a runaway success in the Benelux, Philips has rolled out the Senseo coffee concept worldwide, and is in a hurry to prevent copy-cats from joining the party (when Philips and Sara Lee failed to get the coffee pads patented in the Netherlands, a whole new business sprang up, with retailers and other coffee producers now introducing their own pads for the Senseo).

So there are new shelves out there. Think of a partner that it makes sense for you to work with and co-create. It's beginning to happen everywhere, for example brands like Nike and Apple have got together to develop a running shoe plugged directly into an iPod. Maybe you should be next.

Table 12.22 Senseo

SENSEO	comments	score (%)
REthink	grasped new shopper opportunity	75
REimagine	traditional, but imaginative	75
REstructure	OK	70
RETAILIZATION	**brand co-creation**	73

Guinness: changing the shelf

'The best looking beer in the world.'

In 1759 Arthur Guinness signed a 9,000-year lease for St James's Gate in Dublin, including water rights – and started brewing beer. Two hundred and forty-five years later, 10 million glasses of Guinness are quaffed daily in 150 countries worldwide.

The product can even change the arena – change the shelf. We should always question whether we are on the right shelf today and more importantly whether we are on the right shelf for tomorrow. Guinness realized it needed a new shelf – the supermarket shelf. The trouble was that their product didn't work there.

Once upon a time, the only place to get the authentic taste of GUINNESS® Draught beer was down at your local pub or bar. Then, in the late 1980s, GUINNESS® Draught In Cans brought your local right into your own fridge. Suddenly, cans were cool again. The patented GUINNESS® In-Can System is an ingenious award-winner. A tiny plastic widget jets a stream of bubbles into the GUINNESS® beer when the can is opened. The 'widget' is actually a plastic moulded device that sits at the bottom of a can until it's opened and then releases a little beer and nitrogen, forcing a surge of bubbles that settle to form the tight white head – in short, the perfect pint at home. The result is black, white and beautiful. Eight hundred million widgets can't be wrong. And there is a huge new arena on the supermarket shelf.

Guinness seems to have recently developed a device that will beam a sonic wave through your home-poured pint of Guinness to make it cloudy like the one you had in the pub last night. It's all very simple: buy a special type of Guinness called Surger, buy the Surger device, plug it in after you have kept the beer in the fridge for three hours, pour water on the Surger, then pour your pint at 45 degrees and pop it onto the Surger device. Simple!

The technology is part of Guinness's bid to become 'the best looking beer in the world', said Murray, brewmaster for Guinness in Dublin. The new canned beer is already a hit in Ireland, where it sold 22 million cans in one year (Table 12.23).

Table 12.23 Guinness

GUINNESS	comments	score (%)
REthink	leveraged new channel opportunity	70
REimagine	traditional, but imaginative	70
REstructure	OK	70
RETAILIZATION	changing the shelf	70

Starbucks: being in the people-first business

> We're not in the coffee business serving people, we're in the people business, serving coffee.
>
> Howard Schultz, CEO Starbucks

The Howard Schultz quote mentioned above, 'We're not in the coffee business serving people, we're in the people business, serving coffee', is a great quote, and if you can start to think like him, you will have come a long way in understanding how to deal with the shopper. Shopping fulfils a social function in our lives. It is part of our daily lives as modern people. Through shopping we reflect ourselves in the eyes of the world around us.

Trend people talk about 'being spaces', shopping environments that are centred around the need for social interaction and, more importantly, social integration. People opt for 'the real-life buzz of being spaces' (Trendwatching, 2005). Starbucks is certainly a being space. Walk into Starbucks and check it out for yourself. People are lounging on couches, reading newspapers and drinking their grande lattes.

Think of Barnes & Noble. Is it a book store or a being space? It has in-house coffee shops, topical reading groups and evening poetry readings. There is even a Barnes & Noble University, with courses such as 'Buddhism' and 'Everyday Life and Forensics with Court TV'. Is it a book store or a social destination centred around book shopping?

The place we play in defines our strategy.

Here's another way of making the point. When Starbucks deals with their chain of coffee shops, they deal with a whole set of specific principles, rules and norms that apply if you want to run a successful coffee shop chain business. They deal with a very specific set of competitors both from within and from outside the category and, more importantly, they deal with a very specific coffee shop shopper mindset. So whoever runs the most successful coffee shop business is the one who becomes the coffee shop arena market leader. Moreover, once you master an arena you will be allowed to shape that arena by setting new standards, rules and norms.

However, selling a freshly brewed grande double shot, skinny latte out of a coffee shop is an entirely different game from selling a pack of medium roast decaf coffee from a supermarket shelf – an area they are moving into fast. Or even selling ice cream, chilled espressoshots in a can, flavoured Frappuccino drinks in bottles, tea filterbags, tea latte concentrates, bottled juiced teas or finally coffee-flavoured liqueur from that same supermarket. Starbucks know this because, besides running their global coffee shop business, they sell these products off supermarket shelves. Starbucks are also very aware that they are suddenly finding themselves playing in an entirely different arena, on a very different shelf. And with this comes a whole new set of principles, rules, norms, competitors and shoppers. Every one of Starbucks' supermarket products potentially plays to very different shopper mindsets.

Starbucks, with around 8,000 outlets worldwide, has been a frequent target for anti-globalization protests. It entered the UK market only at the beginning of the millenium and has 400 outlets already. Despite that speed of change, Starbucks has never forgotten it's in the people business first. In Malcolm Gladwell's latest international bestseller *Blink* (2006), he tells the fascinating story of Bob Golomb, a sales director in a New Jersey Nissan dealership who on average sells more than twice as much as the average car salesperson. His success stretches over more than a decade and he has received several awards. Of course, there is a long list of obvious and not so obvious reasons for Mr Golomb's tremendous and long-term success, but specifically two things caught our attention. Trying to describe why he has been so successful, Mr Golomb makes two powerful statements. First, he gave his three simple rules: 'Take care of the customer. Take care of the customer. Take care of the customer': a simple but very relevant focus on the customer – the shopper. The second one is, 'You have to give everyone your best shot', meaning that one should always strive to give every single shopper the best possible shopping experience. That's not a bad benchmark for anybody trying to sell things just like yourself. Starbucks really practises what it preaches (Table 12.24).

Since 1992, its stock has risen a staggering 5,000 per cent! The genius of Starbucks' success lies in its ability to create personalized customer experi-

Table 12.24   Starbucks

STARBUCKS	Comments	Score (%)
REthink	give people what they want philosophy	85
REimagine	imaginative	85
REstructure	internationally exploding	85
RETAILIZATION	**people first**	85

ences, stimulate business growth, generate profits, energize employees, and secure customer loyalty – all at the same time.

The Starbucks experience contains a robust blend of home-brewed ingenuity and people-driven philosophies that have made Starbucks one of the world's 'most admired' companies, according to *Fortune* magazine. With unique access to Starbucks personnel and resources, Joseph Michelli in his new book *The Starbucks Experience* cites five Principles that have turned the Ordinary into the Extraordinary at Starbucks:

1. Reach out to entire communities.
2. Listen to individual workers and consumers.
3. Seize growth opportunities in every market.
4. Custom-design a truly satisfying experience that benefits everyone involved.
5. Never forget it. You are in the people first business if you're in the retail business.

Superquinn: making customers a part of the family

> In our mission statement we don't even talk about profit or return on investment. We're not financially driven at all. We're customer driven.
> Feargal Quinn, Founder and CEO

This incredible and dynamic small Irish chain of supermarkets offers its customers an unrivalled shopping experience. When was the last time you got excited about going to the supermarket? This chain of supermarkets seems to have changed all that. If you've ever been to Superquinn, you'll know what we're talking about. This relatively tiny chain of just 19 stores, situated in and around Dublin's fair city, has completely redefined the grocery shopping experience. It has created a local market leadership position that gets the better of giant competitors like Sainsbury's, Safeway and Tesco.

Make sure it's 'fresh'!

The minute you walk into Superquinn, you know that you're not in an average supermarket. Every store has its own large on-site bakery, an idea that Superquinn pioneered decades ago. And this characteristic feature tells you almost everything you need to know about the company right from the outset. When they call themselves 'the specialists in fresh food', they really mean it. The bread you buy at Superquinn is never more than four hours old. And the best evidence of that is the fact that you can actually see and smell it being baked right there in front of your own eyes by a team of traditional-looking bakers in white caps and overalls.

It's a simple idea, really. And one that's frequently copied by everyone else these days. If your single-minded objective is to stand for the freshest food available, you will prepare fresh food every day in your own specialist in-store delicatessens, pizza and pasta kitchens, salad kitchens and even sausage kitchens. They insist that fruit and vegetables are delivered fresh from the farm on a twice-daily basis and marked with information on when and where they were picked, along with a biography of the grower! Additionally, they also refuse, year after year, to stock non-grocery items because that is inconsistent with the focused core strategy of the company.

REAL customer service

Beyond specializing in fresh food, the second crucial element in the company's core strategy is an almost fanatical approach to customer service. Feargal Quinn – the company's founder and CEO, and the man who put the 'Quinn' in Superquinn, has been called Ireland's 'Pope of Customer Service'. Quinn and his company are living proof that being close to the customer is a highly successful business strategy. Feargal Quinn started out with seven people in 1960 with his first Superquinn store in Dundalk. He was just 23. Today, 40 years on, Superquinn is a company that employs 5,700 people with 19 stores and 8 shopping centres in the greater Dublin area, where their share of the total grocery business is around 20 per cent. This makes Superquinn the clear market leader.

The Boomerang Principle

These facts, although impressive, are not what apparently motivates Feargal Quinn. Quinn is motivated by what he calls the 'Boomerang Principle'. He believes that the name of the game is getting the customer back for repeat business in the longer term, instead of trying to maximize profit from each current transaction. You can see plenty of examples of this principle in practice, starting from the Superquinn Playhouse, which has been one of the company's most famous trademarks for over 20 years. It's a professionally staffed child-care centre where mothers can leave their small children in capable hands while they concentrate on the serious business of shopping. One of his customers told him about the problems of shopping with kids and said if he could do anything about it 'I'd be a loyal customer for life'. Other young mothers were having similar trouble shopping with their children. So, despite the considerable costs involved, he took the decision to install a Superquinn Playhouse as a permanent feature in every store, arguing that it would give customers another reason to shop at Superquinn rather than going to the competitors. Kindergarten teachers around Ireland even talk about 'Superquinn kids', praising their advanced social skills and the fact that they seem more ready for school life than their peers.

Quinn spends most of his week on the shop floor of his various Superquinn stores, talking to customers and employees about the way things are running and how they could be improved. This is 'Management by Walking Around' taken to the limit. And that's why Superquinn feels so much like that little corner grocery store you remember from your childhood – where everything was very personal and the proprietor knew your name – except that it's all on a much grander scale.

Where innovations are born – customer co-creation

Superquinn are the experts at getting their customers involved – co-creating the future with them. Time and time again, Superquinn has been the pioneer, from introducing Wednesday-afternoon opening to the intro-duction of in-store bakeries, staffed specialist counters and Superquinn Playhouses. One customer at his panels complained that in the evening the trays in the salad bar were often half-empty. 'That's because we pride ourselves on never leaving anything over until the next day', Quinn responded. 'It's a demonstration of our "only fresh today" policy.' But the customer was having none of that. He insisted that it looked terrible, and suggested that when the trays became half-empty, the salads should be put into smaller trays. 'That way you won't have your leftovers, but the display will look attractive because the trays will always be full.' This smart, yet simple idea was soon implemented in all the stores.

Superquinn also involved its customers in the redesign of its new, re-cyclable shopping bags, asking them which shapes, sizes and materials they preferred. Only when Quinn was sure that the new bags conformed exactly to the customers' wishes were they introduced, and of course they were very enthusiastically received.

'People think of Superquinn as an innovative company,' Quinn says, as we queue up for coffee in the staff canteen, 'but our objective has never been just to try out new things for the sake of being different. Our goal is to do whatever it takes – and I really mean that; whatever it takes – to offer our customers the freshest food and the most pleasant shopping experience. So our innovations have always come from listening very intensely to our customers, and basically from implementing ideas that they have suggested or inspired.'

These days everyone talks about 'listening to your customers'. It's one of the classic clichés. But very few actually do it. And nobody does it better than Superquinn. They have a system for listening to their customers that is a permanent part of the way they do business. It's embedded in the company's core strategy for achieving competitive advantage and growth. Every two weeks Quinn personally attends a customer panel at one of his stores, where about 12 volunteer shoppers sit down with him for about 90 minutes to discuss their shopping experiences at Superquinn. This direct personal contact with customers gives Quinn and his colleagues a genuine feel for the people who generate their business. It functions as an early warning system on new trends and it identifies issues that are bothering customers. And it reveals excellent opportunities for Superquinn to steal a march on the competition.

Customer panels are just one of the many listening channels that Superquinn employs. Others include customer comment forms; customer service desks, which are helpfully situated near the entrance of the stores; media monitoring to check for hostile or helpful comments in the press; and formal market research for obtaining quantified data. In addition, Superquinn's floor staff wear sweaters that bear the invitation 'May I help you?', which encourages dialogue between customers and staff so that inquiries or complaints can be dealt with directly and positively by the people concerned. Managers are also very accessible to customers. They can usually be found out on the shop floor, providing yet another channel of communication between the customers and the company.

An article in *Fast Company* noted that 'to shop at Superquinn is to feel understood, to see your questions and complaints addressed before you raise them'. Why do you have to pay for the broccoli stalks and carrot tops you never use? At Superquinn, you don't. The store provides scissors at the display, so you can cut off what you don't want. Why can't you ever decipher your receipt? At Superquinn, the checkout technology provides a running tab on a screen that faces the customer, and then organizes the final receipt by product category, rather than by the order in which products were scanned. 'If you want a 10 kg bag of potatoes from the vegetable department, don't bother to lift one into your shopping trolley. Just pick up a bar-coded card and take it to the checkout, where they will arrange for your potatoes to be carried out for you, along with the rest of your shopping.' Every single checkout counter is staffed by two people; one to scan the products and the other to pack your bags, making sure, for example, that meat goes in one bag and dairy products in another.

Superquinn has also introduced high-tech innovations like self-scan shopping, digital shelf labels, mobile checkout technology and multifunctional kiosks that link customers to their bank, to SuperClub (the store's loyalty programme), as well as to wine recommendations and interactive recipe planners. And it's little things too. If it's a rainy day – and Dublin has quite a few of those – customers are just as pleased with the low-tech, complimentary umbrellas at the door and the carry-out service to the car.

Welcome to the 'world class team'

Superquinn's company mission is 'To be a world class team renowned for excellence in fresh food and customer service'. Everybody in the company feels like a member of that 'world class team', which creates a culture where people take pride in their daily work. They want to be 'renowned for excellence' and you can see evidence of that in every corner of the store. Whether a person's job is to bake bread, cut meat, stack shelves or scan food through the checkout counter, these tasks seem to be undertaken with a sense of personal responsibility for upholding Superquinn's lofty standards of 'excellence'.

A couple of years ago they introduced the idea that 'Everybody is a Manager'. So even the 16-year-old who is filling shelves with cans of salmon is recognized as the manager of that particular responsibility. His photograph can be seen right next to the display, with a sign that says he's in charge of canned salmon. His neighbours, relatives or peers can say 'hey, you did a great job there' or 'it wasn't so good today' or whatever. But the important point is that everybody is in charge of something. They are recognized for something. And that motivates people to grow in stature and confidence.

Staying where the action is

True to the idea that 'Everybody is a Manager', Quinn has absolutely no regard for hierarchy. Some years ago, he did away with the term 'Head Office' and replaced it with 'Support Office' to impress on the administrative staff that they were not higher up the corporate ladder than their colleagues in the stores. In fact, quite the reverse. Their role in the organization is to provide support to the most important people in the company – those who deal directly with the customers.

All of Superquinn's top managers have to spend half a day each week in the shops, serving the customers in some way. Why? Quinn says, 'If you are customer driven, the most important place in the company is not the boardroom but the marketplace.' This ensures that the energy of the organization is concentrated in the right place – towards generating customer satisfaction. In his best-selling book *Crowning the Customer*, he writes: 'The centre of gravity of a business should be kept as close as possible to the point where the action is – where the business meets the customer.' That's why Superquinn managers are required to spend time each month 'stepping into the customer's shoes' – actually shopping for their families in the store. This gives them firsthand experience of what it is like to be a Superquinn customer – ordering food at the counters, looking for hard-to-find items, waiting in line at the checkouts. By becoming customers themselves on a regular basis, they get to see things from the customer's perspective instead of from a management perspective. As Quinn likes to remind them, 'the marketplace looks totally different from where the customer is standing'.

He also encourages the idea that everybody is an innovator. Every single Superquinn colleague has access to the company's weekly results – right across the whole chain. They can see how much was sold and where, so they can compare the performance of different supermarkets on a department-by-department basis. Most importantly, they can see how many 'loyal households' were served – that is, members of a household who have returned to shop at the store again and who visited and bought from their own department. And, as you might expect, this is the basis on which Quinn rewards and compensates them. So every employee is challenged to find innovative ways to increase the number of loyal households they are serving. Which is exactly what they do, testing out their ideas right there on the shop floor and getting rapid feedback on the results.

In fact, Quinn really does view his people as the key to Superquinn's success. In comparison with other supermarkets, where staff has typically been cut down to an absolute minimum, the average Superquinn has a disproportionately large number of employees because Quinn believes that 'customers want a high level of human beings rather than machines'. Yet he is able to offer this degree of personal service without charging higher prices because, as he says, 'investing in people pays off in terms of increased business, which in turn pays for the additional staffing costs'. This aspect of Superquinn has understandably attracted much attention from around the world, because it bucks the conventional wisdom that a high-service operation needs to pass on higher prices to the customer.

'Making our customers a part of the family'

Superquinn's loyalty programme, SuperClub, which was launched back in 1993, was Ireland's first loyalty reward scheme in the retail trade. Today, over 450,000 Irish households are members, representing over one-quarter of all the households in Ireland. The club has been set up with a nationwide network of partner companies, including filling stations, DIY stores, bookshops, sport equipment retailers, travel agents and hotels. Every time a SuperClub cardholder purchases goods or services at Superquinn or any of its partners (there are over 250 outlets across Ireland that participate in the scheme), members collect points which can be converted into gifts from the SuperClub catalogue, money-off vouchers for a range of goods and services, or low-cost travel offers. On average, 12,000 gifts are collected by SuperClub members each week. At Christmas, this figure rises to almost 35,000. In total, about $7 million worth of gifts (at retail value) are given away every year, which is clear proof of Quinn's commitment to reward the loyalty of the customer.

Although SuperClub is not exclusively limited to the Superquinn chain, the scheme has done a lot to cement the loyalty of Quinn's customers. 'It's like making our customers a part of the family', he says. Each store manager personally calls hundreds of local SuperClub members every quarter to stay in touch with them and – surprise, surprise – to invite their comments on improving Superquinn's service. Thanks to the card-reading technology, SuperClub members have their name displayed on a screen, so the checkout assistant and bag-packer can greet them by name. Superquinn's employees may already know several hundred customers by sight, but this technique helps them to remember their names, too, which goes a long way towards establishing a personal and friendly rapport. In many cases the checkout assistants – and Quinn too – are actually on first-name terms with their customers.

SuperClub membership also entitles customers to added-value services in the store, like 'SuperScan' which allows them to scan their purchases themselves using a hand-held scanner as they place items into the cart. This saves substantial time at the checkout, where all the customer has to do is pay. I talked to a couple who were actually using this system in the store, and they enthused about how much simpler, easier and faster it made their shopping. If the average Superquinn customer feels loved and adored, then the SuperClub member feels even more so (Table 12.25).

You can sum up the success of Superquinn in a few simple thoughts:

- Focus!
- Be customer driven!

- Listen!
- Have fun!

There truly is nothing like the Superquinn experience.

Table 12.25 Superquinn

SUPERQUINN	comments	score (%)
REthink	customers first	95
REimagine	customer impact maximized	95
REstructure	constantly developing	95
RETAILIZATION	**customer family**	95

Whole Foods Market®: ethics in action

> Simply the best merchandised anywhere.
>
> Sir Martin Sorrell, CEO WPP

Founded in 1980 as one small store in Austin, Texas, Whole Foods Market® is now the world's leading retailer of natural and organic foods, with 189 stores in North America and the United Kingdom. To date, Whole Foods Market remains driven by a very single-minded mission: 'We're highly selective about what we sell, dedicated to stringent quality standards, and committed to sustainable agriculture.'

They go onto say that they believe in a virtuous circle entwining the food chain, human beings and Mother Earth: each is reliant upon the others through a beautiful and delicate symbiosis. Nice words and it seems they practise them.

It's hard to find fault with Whole Foods, the supermarket chain that has made a fortune by transforming grocery shopping into a bright and shiny, progressive experience. Indeed, the road to wild profits and cultural cachet has been surprisingly smooth for the supermarket chain. It gets mostly sympathetic coverage in the local and national media and red-carpet treatment from the communities it enters.

> There's no inherent reason why business cannot be ethical, socially responsible, and profitable.
>
> John Mackey, the company's chairman

Under the umbrella creed of 'sustainability', Whole Foods pays its workers a solid living wage – its lowest earners an average $13.15 an hour – with excellent benefits and health care. No executive makes more than 14 times the employee average. (Mackey's salary in 2006 was $342,000.) In January 2006, Whole Foods announced that it had committed to buy a year's supply of power from a wind-power utility in Wyoming (Culturebox, 2006).

Publix, Giant Eagle, Safeway and Wal-Mart are all trying to replicate the products and experiences Whole Foods delivers, but they can't replicate the people Whole Foods has delivering the products and experiences to customers. Products and programmes do not create brands, people create brands. People matter more in creating a brand than do products or programmes. WFM seems to understand the power of a knowledgeable, caring and passionate workforce in creating highly satisfied customers. They've created a company culture that connects with their team members (employees) and they in turn pass that connection onto WFM shoppers (*USA Today*, 2006).

If one were to take the WFM team member out from its business, Whole Foods Market would not be the successful company it is today. Try saying the same thing for Wal-Mart. That's somewhat more difficult! It shows as well. Look at *Fortune*'s ranking of WFM in recent years as one of the best US companies to work for:

Fortune® 100 Best Companies to Work For
2006 – number 15
2005 – number 30
2004 – number 47
2003 – number 32
2002 – number 48
2001 – number 41
2000 – number 72
1999 – number 48
1998 – number 34

Finally, we think it's worth repeating some of their claims – claims that seem to be constantly praised everywhere. WFM was recently voted the greatest food retailer in the world by the *Grocer* magazine's panel of experts in the UK:

- *Whole Foods*: We obtain our products locally and from all over the world, often from small, uniquely dedicated food artisans. We strive to offer the highest quality, least processed, most flavorful and naturally preserved foods. Why? Because food in its purest state – unadulterated by artificial additives, sweeteners, colourings and preservatives – is the best tasting and most nutritious food available.

- *Whole People*: We recruit the best people we can to become part of our team. We empower them to make their own decisions, creating a respectful workplace where people are treated fairly and are highly motivated to succeed. We look for people who are passionate about food. Our team members are also well-rounded human beings. They play a critical role in helping build the store into a profitable and beneficial part of its community.
- *Whole Planet*: We believe companies, like individuals, must assume their share of responsibility as tenants of Planet Earth. On a global basis we actively support organic farming – the best method for promoting sustainable agriculture and protecting the environment and the farm workers. On a local basis, we are actively involved in our communities by supporting food banks, sponsoring neighborhood events, compensating our team members for community service work, and contributing at least five per cent of total net profits to not-for-profit organizations.

> Staggering range of innovative lines and good food. This is food shopping as a pure leisure activity.
>
> Simon Bell, Retail Director, Leathams

This is a company that has truly made ethics its mantra. And made it work… BIG TIME (Table 12.26).

Table 12.26 Whole Foods Market

WHOLE FOODS MARKET	comments	score (%)
REthink	the world's first	95
REimagine	highly innovative lines and good food	95
REstructure	huge expansion and now going international	95
RETAILIZATION	ethics in action	95

Karmaloop: turning shoppers into fanatics

> First and foremost, we have a lot of interaction with our customers. We have a whole bunch of customers that we've become friends with. They're fanatics, and they give us a lot of feedback.
>
> Greg Selkoe, co-founder of online clothing juggernaut Karmaloop

Specializing in urban fashion, Karmaloop, the US's largest independent seller of cutting-edge urban fashion online, carries such well-known brands as Kangol, Freshjive and Triple Five Soul, as well as lesser-knowns such as Body Bag, House Of Spy and Silent Revolution. For a company that began in 1999, carrying a scant four clothing lines (Snug, Kappa, Gat and Esdjco), Karmaloop.com has successfully built the largest selection of boutique clothing online. Because of its following and reputation for style, Karmaloop have become the spot online to go for cool, hip streetwear. The Karmaloop team prides itself on having the best selection of often difficult-to-find eclectic styles and brands online.

Far more than just an online store, Karmaloop has successfully enhanced their brand partners' identity and visibility within the 18–30 streetwear market. In addition to providing an online retail outlet, Karmaloop provides their brands with professional photo shoots, sales and demographic data, product testing, print and online co-op advertising and various on- and offline promotions. Karmaloop's brand partners include such authentic, original and progressive clothing companies as Spiewak, 3d Innovations, Sensitive and Ben Sherman. In fact, Karmaloop was the first online retailer to carry the revered Ben Sherman line.

Karmaloop helps give their partner brands rapid entrance into the fickle 18–30 early adopters market. With an e-mail list of a million young online shoppers, Karmaloop is able to get their brands in front of these tastemakers where they spend time – online. Examples abound – Fidel, another hot Montreal-based line, is utilizing their relationship with Karmaloop to break into the American market. Sensitive/3d Innovations, a hot Boston-based line, was picked up as a new trend in Japan due to Karmaloop's online global reach.

In addition to their extensive knowledge of cutting-edge urban fashion, the Karmaloop team are all deeply interested in and influenced by the edgiest music. Every day a new CD is given away for free with every order. One CD for example is an Astralwerks sampler (Karmaloop.com).

Karmaloop maintains its successful relationships with its lines though a combination of successful marketing and the independent grass-roots attitude they share. Karmaloop has been able to weather the recent tough times for online retail with its blend of savvy marketing, tasteful buying, and extensive knowledge of its market.

Karmaloop has been progressing in leaps and bounds. It has been an unequivocal success, with about 350,000 visitors a month, 15 full-time employees, and a smattering of part-time and intern employees. Not shabby for a company that started just in 1999, and began undertaking the arduous task of selling clothes on the web in 2000.

Given the fickle nature of fashion, predictions for future styles can be a daunting task. Greg, when he talks about future trends, says, 'Karmaloop's always been set apart by the fact that it's eclectic. Not all of the brands are totally similar, but the underlying thread that ties us together is unique, cutting-edge style. A lot of streetwear is moving in that direction; people aren't being held down by one trend. It's getting more sophisticated. Mixing and matching is such an American philosophy, because it's such an amalgamation of different cultures. People adopt pieces of cultures that reflect this, and have woven them into their look, their feel and their lifestyle.

'There are definitely up-and-coming brands that don't have as much of a following', he continues. 'We have a brand called Tank Theory, which has some really cool t-shirt designs. Penguin is a hot new brand that's doing well in a lot of places, but most people haven't caught on yet. I'm sure they will.'

Karmaloop has just begun to expand their creative reach, carrying Japanese toys. 'Basically, I wanted to get as many free toys as I could', Greg says with a laugh. 'They're cool. A lot of people, a lot of toyheads in the office thought that people would be interested.' Have people picked up on them yet? 'It started off slow, but the word's been spreading. It's only been about a month, but it's catching on.'

Karmaloop works in one of the most difficult industries in the world – street fashion. Here today and definitely gone tomorrow. By turning its customers into real fanatics who are involved in the company, it looks like surviving the fickle and transient nature of their industry. Not bad for a retail brand (Table 12.27).

Table 12.27 Karmaloop

KARMALOOP	Comments	Score (%)
REthink	urban fashion online	85
REimagine	highly innovative lines and brands	85
REstructure	yet to be proven	70
RETAILIZATION	**turning shoppers into fanatics**	80

Our retail winners: who, why and how

Retailizing your business is not a static achievement, but a dynamic process. We have provided you with a guide – a process and 25 case studies to help you develop your thinking and actions. But in the end the decision to retailize is yours and yours alone. Do you want to seize the Retailization opportunity? Do you want to retailize? Do you want to survive? Do you want to live, breathe and think retail in everything you do? Do you want to regain power? It's up to you!

So did our cases get it right? They sure did (Table 12.28).

Score your retailization efficiency based on these cases:

- How do you stack up?
- Do you REthink, REimagine and REstructure your retail efforts?
- Do you retailize?

Table 12.28 Our retail winners

Retail brand winner	Winning strategy	Retailization score
Yoyamart	a brand that understands the situation	63
Gooh!	reinventing the boring!	63
Innocent	staying innocent	77
Holland & Holland	making more of more	70
REI	living the brand experience	70
Dyson	innovation leads the way	77
Zara	react rather than predict	90
Bose	try, try and try again	67
Tchibo	creating an unchallenged 'star'	67
Oliviers and Co.	creating wants, not needs	67
Apple	total involvement	99
easyJet	creating choice where there's no choice	77
Red Bull	rewriting the rules	83
Procter & Gamble	the moments of truth	95
Gillette	constant innovation	77
ASSA ABLOY	solve a problem	77
Peroni	challenging perceptions	70
H&M	four seconds to get them!	90
Courvoisier	REvitalization	79
Senseo	brand co-opetition	73
Guinness	changing the shelf	70
Starbucks	being in the people-first business	85
Superquinn	making customers a part of the family	95
Whole Foods Market	ethics in action	95
Karmaloop	turning shoppers into fanatics	80

Succeeding in the future

In peace prepare for war, in war prepare for peace.

Sun Tzu

One thing in life and business is certain. We are all travelling towards the future at 60 minutes per hour, no matter what we do or who we are. We are all going to arrive there no matter what. What is the future of your business? How can you prepare for it?

All human experience is expansive and omni-directional, including the future. Because the future is not linear, you cannot prepare for it with one single plan, one single solution. To harvest the profits in the future you should have several alternative plans based on improbable as well as probable future events. If you only have one scenario and it goes wrong, you have a problem.

It is one of the strange facts of experience that when we try to think into the future our thoughts also jump backwards. It may well be that nature has some fundamental law by which opening up the future opens up the past to a certain extent. When you look into the future your forward-looking and backward-looking thinking combine like two twists of rope, and intertwine round each other inextricably. Therefore, when you think about the future of your retail business, you also force yourself to think about what is happening in your business now and what happened in the past. If you do not plan for the future, you may end up like the farmer who over-farmed his land to the point that he couldn't even raise his voice on it.

Hopefully, by taking you through 25 case studies have shown you a bit of someone's successful past and maybe a bit of your successful future. Then your future can be more of a guaranteed success.

When you look at our cases (Figure 12.29) you can see that one brand tops the list in terms of retailization efficiency – Apple, followed closely by another brand, P&G (or maybe 17 brands). Then comes a series of classic retailers from Whole Foods Market to H&M, followed by more classic brands.

People are always fearful of forecasting the future, because they are invariably wrong. Events have a habit of overtaking the extrapolations. However, some things seem more certain than others. Retailers will continue to grow, consolidate and dominate the marketplace. Consumers will increasingly grow in scepticism, both about the products they buy and what they're told about them. Private label will become more and more acceptable as quality and price perceptions erode. Communications will continue to fragment and become more and more niche in nature. An even more squeezed brand is the inevitable result. The squeezed brand will continue to be squeezed until it reaches the point of near-explosion. We need to ensure we can survive the squeeze. We need to ensure we can prosper.

Marketers must ask themselves: 'Is making retail work the single biggest issue in my business? Forget about writing the long-term strategies for my brand – I must write the retail strategy for my business. I must learn to sell again!' Retailers must ask themselves: 'Are we making the best of our

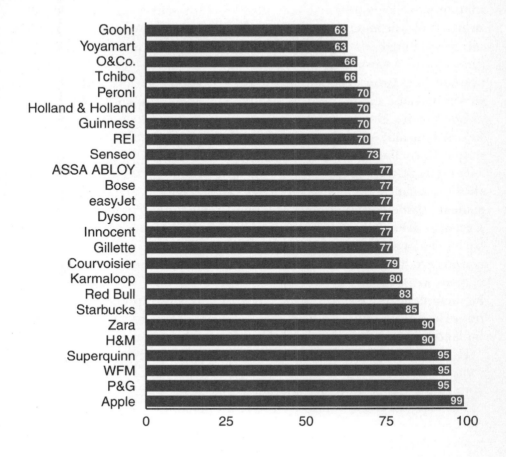

Figure 12.29 Retailization efficiency scores (%)

strategy? Are we making the best of our brands? Are we making the best of our relationships? Are we creating and co-creating enough?'

Despite all these questions, we should never forget one thing: **It's about shopping, stupid!** The verb 'to be' has been replaced with the verb 'to have' as we move towards the 'me' shopper we described earlier – a shopper who wants more, and wants more his or her way. We shop… therefore we are. We supply… therefore we are!

The yellow brick road to the consumer has become very long and very winding. Retail is the medium that will bridge the gap and straighten the road to the consumer or, more relevantly, the shopper. This is the medium where brand selection takes place. This is the medium where retail communications become the 'only' important way to communicate. Shopping is where it happens! You have to focus on the point of action – the point where shoppers really get involved – the point of brand selection. The reward for dealing with the issue is the ultimate reward for any brand: loyalty. Loyalty means sustained sales. Loyalty means growth. Loyalty means a future. We are living in a world where everyone searches for the next sale. Retail is fundamentally critical because no matter how hard you work at developing products and brands, there's little point if you can't sell them to your ultimate consumer.

Now you may be asking yourself, 'Why do I need to learn from retail winners?' We'll tell you. The current world of retail is a 'jungle'. It exists in a state of absolute chaos. Thanks to modern technology, thousands on thousands of retailers are vying for attention in a limited marketplace. With ordinary strategies, you simply will not succeed.

Here is a simple fact: to stand out in the modern retail environment, you have to be extraordinary. Our case studies of elite retail winners hopefully provide you with some thoughts about what you need to be extraordinary, not just ordinary!

Now we get to you. And one way to help you is to provide you with a route map for the future, an operational methodology that will identify the right road(s) and steer you down them. Read on.

Part 3

How to succeed operationally

13 A source of light

We start by imagining the brand as a source of light. Traditionally, as we described earlier, that source of light has been pointed towards consumers, with the objective of building brand preference and ultimately purchase. However, this objective has become increasingly meaningless, as the power of mass communications has fragmented and eroded, and the ultimate consumer has developed from a passive consumer watching television to an active shopper seeking the best he or she can get. But we shouldn't have stopped with the consumer (Figure 13.1).

Our real target market was the shopper – someone we have often failed to reach. Our obsession with the consumer has caused us to miss the real target audience – the shopper. We need new sources of focus to enable us to reach the shopper again and again. Those foci are, of course, the seven stages of retailization (Figure 13.2).

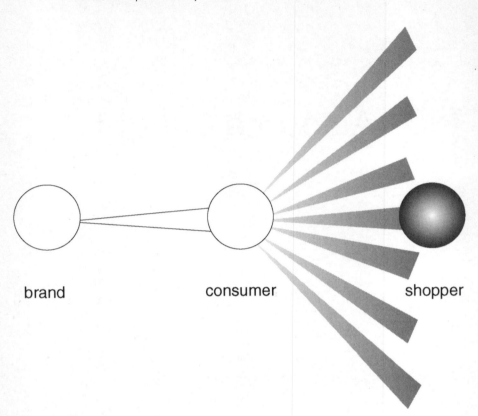

Figure 13.1 The lost shopper

Those sources of focus or lens are our seven stages, which are grouped into three mindsets: REthink, REimagine and REstructure – *mindsets that allow us to focus on the retail issues that matter*.

Let's look at those mindset objectives in more detail.

Starting with the REthink mindset, we cover the first three stages of the retailization process where we need insights, breakthrough research and alternative perspectives to help us fully understand the arenas within which we operate, the competitive context within which we exist and finally the way our shoppers interact with our category and its products. The process starts with the arena, by asking: Where do we create our sale(s)? Which shelf do we sit on and which one should we sit on? Having defined our arenas, we move on to the competitive context and ask who else is generating sale(s) in that arena. Who else is on the shelf next to us? Only by understanding them can we define how to steal their sale(s). Next we move on to the shopper, as we try to understand what exactly defines shopping in

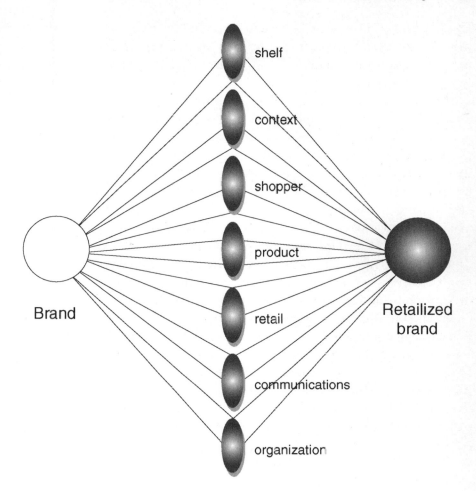

shelf

context

shopper

product

retail

communications

organization

Brand

Retailized
brand

Figure 13.2   The focused retailized brand

our category and how people shop there. What makes them buy? What will make them buy?

Once we have rethought, we need to start REimagining: re-imagining what we sell and how we sell it. We need to start (re)-creating great products and great retail experiences, creating product and shopping experiences that will excel during the two moments of truth. Simply said, products that are exciting to buy and equally exciting to try – buying and trying – creating sale(s). In product conception we try to understand the very nature of what we are trying to sell, and identify what would create the optimal sale(s). Based on our understanding from Steps 1–3 we are able to define how we create the perfect vehicle for sale(s), the perfect product. But a product does not exist in a vacuum. It will always find itself in some sort of retail context, and in Step 5 we try to make the most out of this context. Retail impacting will focus on the importance of extending the product idea into a great shopping experience. Step 5 deals with how we want to create our sale(s).

After having rethought and re-imagined, we need to REstructure, changing the way we approach communications and how we organize ourselves. We need to create communications that will drive shoppers to our products and our shopping experiences. We need to create communications that will help us achieve our sale(s). But none of the stages will work unless we can restructure our organizations and people in order to make everyone live and breathe retail every day. Is your organization geared for retailization? What demands does retailization put on the way you structure yourself? Is retail a major concern for your company? Retailization demands new ways of thinking that lead to new ways of acting. In organizational enhancement, we will try to inspire you to change your organization's attitude and priorities in order to think and act with a great deal more sale(s) focus.

Apart from our three original mindsets we have added two more. The first of these is REeducate, where we use all the knowledge and information we have gleaned from the first three mindsets to build a detailed retail vision. In order to educate our workforce it is necessary to construct a series of toolkits to cascade that message through our organizations.

Finally, we need to recognize that this is not a one-off process, but a continuous one. The REevolve mindset recognizes this need. To summarize:

- REthink
  - Step 1: Understanding our shelf
  - Step 2: Stealing choice
  - Step 3: Leveraging our shopper knowledge
- REimagine
  - Step 4: Maximizing product impact
  - Step 5: Maximizing retail impact
- REstructure
  - Step 6: Communicating with our shoppers
  - Step 7: Retailizing our organization
- REeducate
  - Step 8: Building the vision
  - Step 9: Identifying and specifying the retail vision
  - Step 10: Education and dissemination of the retail vision
- REevolve
  - Step 11: Evolving the retail vision

Let us move from a conventional brand to a retailized brand. You may believe you are already covering all seven steps, and you most probably are. However, we believe our process will add a new rigour and creative and intellectual intensity to an issue that merits it. Retailization is not a pick-and-mix kind of process. You must thoroughly complete all of the steps to reach the objectives and embrace retailization as the long-term guiding philosophy to take you along the pathway to better sale(s) (Figure 13.3).

retailization™ **REthinkREimagineREstructure REeducateREevolve**

Figure 13.3

Let's look at those steps one by one and define what you need to do. What you need to do to REtailize your brand.

14 REtailizing the brand

REthink – Step 1: Understanding our shelf

REthink

The shelf is at the beginning of everything and every single shelf represents an arena that has a unique set of opportunities and challenges that define our strategic perspectives and resulting actions.

Understanding our shelf – key points to be addressed

- Define your shelves – your arenas.
- Define the way those shelves are structured.
- Define the main shelf challenges you face.
- Identify the means to meet those challenges.
- Evaluate and optimize your selection of the shelves you want to be on.
- Decide whether you're fighting on the right shelves today.
- Start exploring alternative shelf opportunities, from the internet to concept stores.
- Consider creating your own unique shelves.
- Consider reinventing the shelves you're already on.
- Consider if there are any possibilities for co-opetition that will maximize shelf opportunities.

REstorm tools (retail brandstorming tools)

a   Describe how your brand would look on any of these shelves (Figure 14.1).
b   Describe in words and pictures the ideal concept store for your brand. Try to construct a three-dimensional representation of what it might look like and what it's trying to tell your shoppers about you.

present	**internet**	**concept**
cooperative	**reinvention**	**off the planet**

Figure 14.1 Shelf possibilities matrix

REthink – Step 2: Stealing choice

REthink

In a world of infinite choices you have no choice, but to steal choice from whoever you can. Our competitive context therefore defines our opportunities

Stealing choice – key points to be addressed

- Map out your competitive context using the retail orientation grid.
- Define their strengths and their weaknesses and yours.
- Embrace the ideology of stealing choice.
- Identify ways to steal choice.
- Get inspired by other categories.
- Define how you can become the chosen one.
- Use a problem detection study to identify the gaps and holes in the competitive context.
- Start building real ideas and concepts based on the failures of everyone else in your category.
- Create a long-term objective based programme for constant out-innovation of your competitive context.
- See if you can create real choice in areas of the category where choice has been forgotten or neglected or never even existed.

REstorm tools

a Where are your key competitors? Where are you and where do you want to be? When you consider your brand as an impulse purchase, where are you? When you consider your brand as a considered purchase, where are you? (Figure 14.2)

b Tug of war exercise. The grid shown in Figure 14.3 helps you do the following:

1 better define your challenges;
2 identify strengths you can maximize;
3 identify strengths you can minimize.

Try assembling a grid for your retail challenge. Your tug of war.

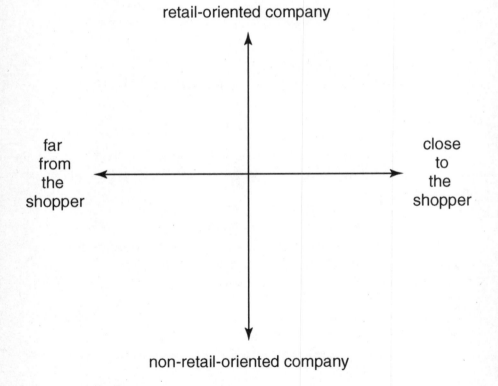

Figure 14.2 Retail orientation grid

TUG OF WAR			
Challenge: probability of getting a major sale			
winning the sale	+	–	losing the sale
superior	◄ product		inferior
none		competition ►	superior
lowest	◄ shopper need	price ►	highest
real	◄ shopper knowledge		little or none
high	◄ shopper budget		low
able to buy			not able to buy
excellent		sales presentation ►	poor
able to overcome	◄ answering objections		not able to overcome
liked by shopper		shopper compatibility ►	disliked by shopper

Figure 14.3 Tug of war
Source and inspiration: Thinkertoys

REthink – Step 3: Leveraging the shopper

REthink

In a world where shopping has become the world's number one leisure activity you have to reconnect with customers when they shop for your brand. Sale(s) and margin growth will inevitably result

Leveraging our shopper knowledge – key points to be addressed

1. Define your consumers as shoppers.
2. Define your shoppers as situiduals, ie what typical situations are they in when they shop for your brands?
3. Identify what other types of products they're shopping for when they shop for you.
4. Collate all your shopper data to date. What do you really know about your shoppers and their buying behaviour?
5. Determine what kind of experience they are looking for.
6. Identify the solutions they need in order to make their shopping more convenient, productive and pleasurable.
7. Analyse how the shopper would define the shelf, the competitive context and even themselves.
8. Determine how the shopper would define the ideal shopping situation – pre, during and post the experience.
9. Based on your immediate understanding of the shopper, determine how you would put people first in your offering.
10. Based on your immediate understanding of the shopper, see if you can turn your offering into a want, rather than a need.

REstorm tools

a   Thinking of your shoppers, ask yourself three basic questions (Figure 14.4). Then ask yourself what you'd change as a result.
b   Draw a picture of your brand as you see it. Draw another picture of your brand as the shopper sees it (Figure 14.5).
c   List the key shopping stimuli for your brand at each stage of the shopping experience (Figure 14.6). Think about how you can affect every one of them and build action plans to do so.

What do shoppers *need* from you?	?	?	?
What do shoppers *want* from you?	?	?	?
What can you do to answer that want?	?	?	?

Figure 14.4   Three basic questions

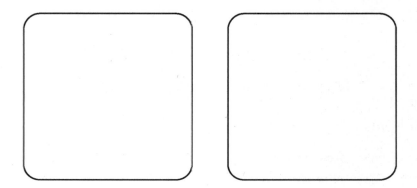

Figure 14.5   Draw your brand as you and the shopper see it

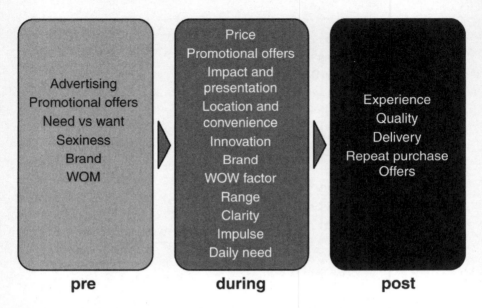

Figure 14.6   Brand shoppability™ during the shopping experience

REimagine – Step 4:
Maximizing product impact

REimagine

Behind every great brand there's a great product. It pays to create a product revolution rather than an evolution.

Maximizing product impact – key points to be addressed

- Having rethought the shelf, the competitive context and the shopper, identify what characterizes the ideal product concept.
- Define what kind of RSP you would like the product concept to stand for.
- Define how you would make your product stand out.
- Define what kind of perspectives there are for its constant remaking.
- Identify routes to making it more than just the core product.
- Make sure it makes sense.
- Identify how you would make it theirs – a RE-me product.
- Define how you would make them beg for it.
- Create the perfect product concept.

REstorm tools

When it comes down to the retail arena, shoppers reach out for products. Make sure that you can offer one for them to reach out for; make sure they reach out for yours. You see, everybody these days has a brand, but very few have a product. It is imperative that everybody involved in product development recognizes the impact of the product in their retail environments:

- Think of your products and the way they perform at retail.
- Give them marks out of 10 for each of clarity, clear RSP, standing out, capable of being more, potential personalization and begability:
  - Clarity (how visible is your product, does it pass the four-second attention test?)
  - Clear RSP (do shoppers get it and will it initiate creative execution?)
  - Standing out (are you unique enough?)
  - Capable of being more (how extendable is the product and where?)
  - Potential personalization (can it meet the needs of niche and mass markets?)
  - Begability (will you produce product fans?)

Add up your total score out of a potential 60 and assess your strengths and weaknesses.

REimagine – Step 5: Maximizing retail impact

REimagine

Shoppers are only loyal to superior shopping experiences.

Maximizing retail impact – key points to be addressed

- Define what would most encourage sale(s) on your shelf.
- Define what makes brands shoppable on your shelf.
- Define what barriers and problems the shoppers experience in your arena and ask yourself whether your product offerings are able to solve these at retail level.
- Define what your competition does better than you.
- Describe in pictures and words what kind of ideal flagship store you would create to cater for your shoppers.

- Define how you can keep your offerings fresh and ahead of the game.
- Define how you can make your unique product offering into a unique retail presence.
- Look for ideas to maximize the buying and trying of your product at retail.
- Make sure your product passes the 'four second' test.
- Create clarity and involvement in the purchase situation.
- Construct a revolutionary and superior shopping situation around your brand offering.

REstorm tools

Use the retail circle of opportunity to identify and explore impact possibilities (Figure 14.7).

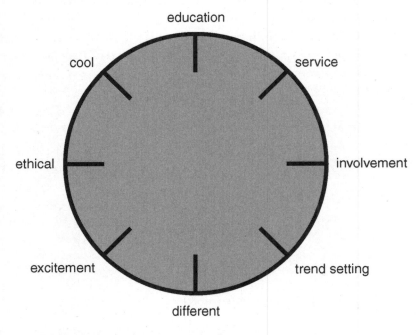

Figure 14.7 Retail circle of opportunity

REstructure – Step 6:
Communicating to shoppers

REstructure

Unique new ways to reach and communicate to our shopper are increasingly available.

Communicating to our shoppers – questions to be addressed

1. Evaluate your overall communication objectives and spending with respect to getting the attention of shoppers.
2. Evaluate your spending's cost-effectiveness against the shopping experience (pre, during and post).
3. Construct a RSP for your brand.
4. Identify your dream communication scenario.
5. See if there's a tryvertising angle to your communication efforts.
6. Determine whether your can BUZZR up your marketing efforts.
7. Analyse whether you can subculturize your brand.
8. Create a community around shopping for your products.
9. Find a BRI – big retail idea.

REstorm tools

a   The RSP briefing form (Retail Selling Proposition):
   – Shelf: what new thinking have you developed? Are there new shelves?
   – Context: what new thinking have you developed to better compete?
   – Shopper: what new thinking/insights have you how developed about your shopper?
   – Product: what have you re-imagined?
   – Retail: describe your revolutionary selling situation.
   – Communications: what communications approaches do you recommend to excite your shoppers and drive them to your shelves?
   – Organization: what changes and structures are you putting in place to retailize your organization?
   – BRI: a simple phrase that captures the essence of your big retail idea.
b   Think of our big retail idea techniques (Figure 14.8) and work out which ones are most useful for your needs, and how you might apply them.

Figure 14.8   The BRI proprietary techniques

REstructure – Step 7:
Retailizing your organization

REstructure

Living, breathing and acting the philosophy of retailization to realize sale(s).

Retailizing your organization – key questions to be addressed

- Create an operational plan for the implementation of your Retailization process.
- Define goals, benchmarks and deadlines.
- Identify a core Retailization team responsible for carrying the process through.

- Create a plan for how to make your organization more retail-curious and how to act on that curiosity.
- Create a plan for incentivizing your organization to be creative and innovative in all matters relating to retail.
- Get everybody involved.
- Define how things will be different.
- Make a long-term commitment for living and breathing Retailization.
- Get going!

REstorm tools

Think of how your organization can involve your brand with your customers – pre, during and post the shopping experience (Figure 14.9).

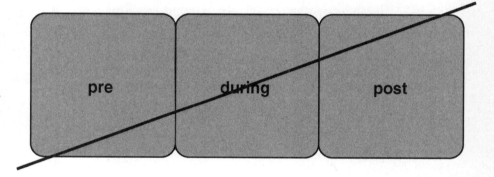

Figure 14.9 Brand involvement activity

Then decide what you would need to change to make it happen.

REeducate – Step 8:
Building the retail vision

REeducate

We believe that in order for the vision to be successfully communicated at all points of contact, every 'brand communicator' must know what the vision is and how to interpret it to his/her own constituency. We educate those communicators of the brand in the power of retail thinking – in the power of REeducation.

Building the retail vision – what we need to know

Once we have fully explored our retailization potential in the previous seven steps we are in a position to pull all this together within a new vision – a retail vision. We need to start by fully understanding our vision background and territory:

- What exactly is our retail brand?
  - Business definition
  - Territory
- Who are we?
  - Retail brand personality
  - Tone/voice/look/feel
- Essential equities
  - Core values we transmit at retail level:
    intrinsic functional values (the basic functional values)
    expressive image values (the values that you make people feel like)
    central driving values (the essence of your retail brand)
- Leverageable assets
  - Brand background
  - Brand properties
  - Givens/mandatories
- Retail brand idea
  - Key creative thought (the BRI)
- How far are we retailized?

REeducate – Step 9:
Identifying and specifying the retail vision

Our retail vision process

Our model for creating the vision makes use of our combined experience, gathered over many years. It has been progressively refined to yield an approach that we have found to be rigorous and disciplined without compromising insightfulness and creativity. We start by maintaining that a retail vision is very different from a brand vision. It is in essence the realization of your brand vision in your retail environments.

Our vision process uses key building blocks: Retail Vision, Retail Mission, Retail Area of Competence, Retail Values and Retail Brand Idea:

- Retail Vision: the world as the brand sees it.
- Retail Mission: mission in the world, based on the retail vision.
- Retail Ambition: how we want the brand to be perceived by the shoppers.
- Retail Area of Competence: the territory of the shelf (or shelves) within which the brand is performing.
- Retail Core Values: what really makes shoppers buy.
- Retail Brand Idea: what you communicate to the shopper – the BRI.

REeducate – Step 10:
Retail vision education and dissemination

REeducate

We believe that it in order for the vision to be successfully communicated at all points of contact, every 'brand communicator' must know what the vision is and how to interpret it to his/her own constituency. We educate those communicators of the brand in the power of retail thinking – in the power of REeducation.

Approval
We need to initiate a series of steps to get the message approved and out.

Preparation of 'Vision report'

- Draft of Retail Vision (with all supporting materials) submitted for approval.
- Make it available on secure internet site as a mechanism to stimulate feedback.
- Ensure approval is secured.
- Introduction at top-management forum.
- Final approval.

Retail brand toolbox launch and dissemination

The retail brand toolbox, of which the retail brand vision is the heart, is our resource for educating all retail brand communicators on the content and use of the retail brand vision and guidelines on how to interpret it to all points of retail contact the brand has with the world.

The primary tool is a retailization brand book from which all educational tools should be cut. The brand book will:

- chronicle the retail brand journey;
- summarize the information found in steps 1 to 7;
- be modular; adapted for each audience;
- be published in an intranet version;
- be updatable.

Launch and dissemination

For maximum impact we recommend staging a launch event that will represent the first of a series of retail brand forums.

Training is about getting the tools into the hands of the brand communicators and teaching them how to maximize the potential of these tools.

Educational initiatives must be reviewed regularly to achieve and maintain optimization.

REevolve – Step 11: Evolving retailization

REevolve

Continuous evolution of the retail vision

Retailization isn't a one-off process. We need to ensure that continuity is not only maintained, but measured and developed over time to ensure a continuous cultivation of our retail vision (Figures 14.10 and 14.11).

Figure 14.10 Retailization model: summary

REthink			REimagine		REstructure	
We believe that it is necessary to rethink the basic fundamentals of retail marketing strategy if the brand is to be truly revitalized			We believe that it is necessary to re-imagine the product and retail execution		We believe that it is necessary to restructure in order to live and breathe retail	
Step 1: Understanding our shelf	Step 2: Stealing choice	Step 3: Leveraging shopper knowledge	Step 4: Maximizing product impact	Step 5: Maximizing retail impact	Step 6: Communicating to shoppers	Step 7: Retailizing the organization
Area of enquiry - Current shelf audit - Future shelf review and analysis	**Area of enquiry** - Current competitive audit - Stealing choice analysis	**Area of enquiry** - Shopper profile focus-group-based review - Situtidual analysis	**Area of enquiry** - Product retail effectiveness assessment	**Area of enquiry** - Retail experience effectiveness assessment	**Area of enquiry** - Current communications impact review and analysis	**Area of enquiry** - Organizational empowerment assessment
Deliverables Shelf exploitation opportunities • Proprietary distribution • Re-invention • Co-opetition	**Deliverables** Choice strategy routes • Building on failure • Creating choice • Out-innovate	**Deliverables** Shopper targetting methodologies • People first • Wants, not needs • Situiduals	**Deliverables** Product development routes • Clarity • USP (RSP) • Standing out • Remake • Make it more • Make sense • Make it personal • Make them beg	**Deliverables** Retail impact programmes • Keep it fresh • Extend the idea • Merge buy and try • Create clarity and involvement	**Deliverables** Communication methodologies • Tryvertising • BUZZR • Subculturize • Building communities	**Deliverables** Empowerment programmes • Get curious • Get creative • Get producting • Get involved • Get moving • Retailize

REeducate
We believe that in order for the vision to be successfully communicated at all points of contact every 'brand communicator' must know what the vision is and how to interpret it to his/her own constituency. We educate those communicators of the brand in the power of retail thinking, in the power of re-education

REevolve
Continuous evolution of the retail brand

Step 8: Building the retail vision		Step 9: Identifying and specifying the retail vision		Step 10: Retail vision education and dissemination		Step 11: Ongoing cultivation
The building blocks	Deliverables	Preparation of 'Vision report'	Deliverables	Retailization tool box	Deliverables	
- What is our retailized brand? - Business definition - Territory **- Who are we?** - Retail brand personality - Tone/voice/look/feel **- Essential equities** - Core values **Leverageable assets** - Brand background - Brand properties - Givens/mandatories	Draft retail brand vision	**- Draft of retail brand vision (with all supporting materials) submitted for approval** - Available on internet site - Feedback mechanism in place **- Approval secured**	Retail brand vision	**- Create the retail brand tool box, including Retailization manual** **- Develop strategy for dissemination**	Retailization tool box Retailization manual Launch plan	- Refresh - Update - Track - Review - Execute

Figure 14.11 Retailization model: summary

15 Postscript... eat or be eaten!

Well. Where are we? Where has our global journey taken us?

We believe it has taken us to a new world with a new ocean. It's clear that this new world has some big fish and some little fish. The biggest fish of them all is the global retailer. This new breed of super-retailer increasingly gets their way, whether they're a food retailer, electronics or DIY. They can decide to swim with the small fish or simply gobble them up and spit them out.

The little fish are of course the brands. There was a time when they were as big as the biggest fish. Now they're a mere reflection of them – a pale reflection of a spectacular success. The big fish have been allowed to conquer the oceans. They were simply the best when it came to surviving. They've constantly grown, developed their abilities and successfully understood their environments. They've understood their shoppers like never before and serviced them with increasingly better-value propositions. They've been really great examples of great businesses, from Zara to Tesco.

But you don't get something for nothing. You can't constantly increase your value offering without becoming more efficient. Some of that efficiency has clearly come from better and better operations. But most of that efficiency has had to be gained from their suppliers. Not suppliers in the raw material traditional sense, but suppliers in the finished product sense. They're suppliers are the very things they sell – their brands.

How times change! They didn't used to be suppliers: they used to be partners – brand partners. Our brands have lost inertia and gained apathy. Many live in their past brand glories and have refused to move on in a world that has moved on. Their same old formulaic offerings have repeatedly risen to the surface whenever they wish to talk to the big fish: 'We can offer line extensions to our retailers, they'll love it and give us more shelf space. We're bound to sell more.'

The problem is that the partner isn't listening any more. Retailers used to listen to their brands in the days when brands knew their customers best – the days when mass communications was the accepted norm to talk to consumers. Now the big fish know everyone's customers best – the shopper has become their knowledge property. Their knowledge has given them strength, given them power, given them confidence – the confidence to say no to line extensions, the confidence to say no to brands, the confidence to have their own small fish: private label, the confidence to use their power.

The dividing line between confidence and arrogance is of course fairly small and some of our big fish (the retailers) have exhibited the latter trait when it comes to dealing with their former partners (the brands). The brands haven't helped themselves when they could have, constantly using tired old formulas to maintain their position instead of trying to leap out of the water to find new oceans or forging relationships that are mutually symbiotic and mutually beneficial. You only have to think of the way sucker fish latch onto big fish like sharks. They get a free ride while eating the shark's pests. Surely there are lessons to be learnt.

The big fish have realized where the food really is – where the power really is. They get it – the power's on the shelf. If you control the shelf, you control the shopper. It's a simple as that. You become the choice master. You determine what people choose, the prime key for growth. You can control choice or, as the French shark would put, 'in a world of choice, there's increasingly no choice – *plus ça change*'.

While you're controlling the shelf you can of course control the profitability of that shelf. You can grow and stay fit at the same time. One way for you to control the shelf profitably is private label. With the increasing global acceptance of private label you have less and less need to worry about the brands. You have your own little fish and they're increasingly profitable in nature. Premium private label is an increasingly attractive option for retailers. As consumer acceptance for private label grows and, more importantly, quality perceptions start to match brand levels, you increasingly have the ultimate strategic control weapon in your hands: great products (we can even call them brands) at great profits. Maybe we'll keep a few brands alongside them just so our shopper can see what a great buy they're getting. Anyway, we need the brands to make these premium products. We need to control them somehow. So we'll let them have a little shelf space.

So what can our brand fish do? Can they survive the next 10 years or are they consigned to the few shelves they're allowed to occupy, as the retailers' reminder to you – the shopper, that you still have a choice. Just please don't take it! Not that you're likely to, with only one in five of you prepared to change store if your favourite brand isn't there. It seems that retailer loyalty has replaced brand loyalty. Convenience wins over loyalty when it comes to the rub.

The first thing the brand owners need to realize is that not all retailers are the same. There are some who will continue to chew you up and there are others waiting for you to wake up. They are the enlightened ones. They realize it's not them or you – it's us. You really do need each other. BRANDS NEED RETAILERS AND RETAILERS NEED BRANDS. When retailers and brands truly work together is when the shelf truly takes on a power and potential of its own. Cooperate or be delisted becomes the new mantra. Cooperate with the retailer and achieve the same objective – sale(s). Don't cooperate and face the very real possibility of delistment. Cooperation is more than a word – it's a proactive investment. Retailers expect brand cash. Brands must start to think of retail as a major investment priority and one that above all supplies a meaningful measure of return on investment. Brands should expect and demand a 'true' partnership as a result.

Finally there's the brand itself. Can we re-brand the brand? Can we give a retail dimension to a conventional brand? We believe that it is more than just possible, either through the age of new communication methods like buzzr or tryvertising or simply repositioning the brand better through the development of powerful RSPs. Fortunately for the brand, their day of opportunity may have arrived. The very concept of the brand is transforming – from branding to the shelf to branding from the shelf. As we said, the shelf is where the power is – all you need to do is own it. Not just own it though, but turn it into the ultimate communication experience. Put the action that surrounds the sale of your product at the forefront of your marketing thinking.

Buying and trying – the two moments of truth that dictate whether your brands live or die. Those two moments are the points of time and contact where you can realize the full retail potential of your brand. Those two moments that bring your shelf alive. Those two moments that will fundamentally change the way you do business in the future, from the way you communicate to your customers to the way you create products to the way you organize your company. We simply need to try. Just remember you've got four seconds to make it work, four seconds to turn the shopper Kings and Queens in your direction, four seconds to confirm their decisions, four seconds to get and secure a sale.

Very finally there's creativity. Co- creation is a tool you should be seizing to bring your retail potential alive and kicking. Co-creation with shoppers in order that you give them the sort of products they really want – the sort of products they will demand from their retailers. Then there's co-creation with retailers, working together to genuinely build and grow the key categories on their shelves.

Well, we started by talking about an ocean, an ocean full of big fish, big retailers. We ended by talking about an ocean of opportunity – an ocean we call the Retailization ocean. Retailization – our new philosophy that attempts to completely refocus your organization and communication efforts, to help you influence your future sales, to help you win your consumers – again and again. To help you reconnect with your ultimate consumer – the shopper. To help you reconnect with your key partners – the retailers. Do you want to swim with the big fish? Do you want to retailize? Do you want to survive? Do you want to eat or be eaten?

The best and only way is to learn more, learn what makes great brands become great retailers (Figure 15.1). We hope this book has shown you a few examples of this in action. It can be done. It isn't a lottery out of your control. It's knowledge that makes the real difference. Please use our strategies, cases, tools and methodologies to help you succeed at retail – again and again.

Good luck and goodnight!

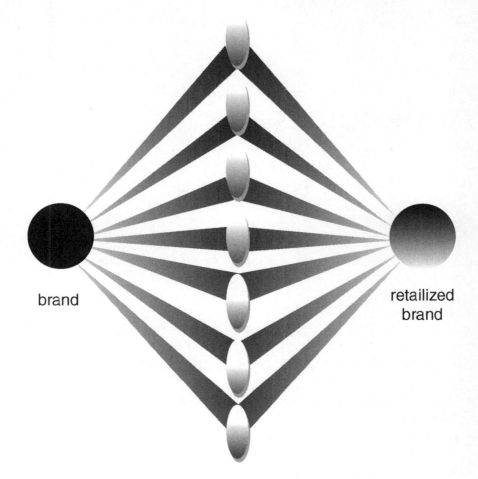

Figure 15.1 The retailized brand

Appendices

We went to a bookstore recently and said to the saleswoman, where's the self-help section? She said, 'if I told you it would defeat the purpose'.

Appendix 1:
How to succeed by being in a RE world

- RETAILIZATION: connecting brands to shoppers through the power of retail thinking.
- REthink: we believe that it is necessary to rethink the basic fundamentals of retail marketing strategy if the brand is to be truly revitalized.
- REimagine: we believe that it is necessary to re-imagine the product and retail execution.
- REstructure: we believe that it is necessary to restructure in order to live and breathe retail.
- REeducate: we believe that it in order for the vision to be successfully communicated at all points of contact every 'brand communicator' must know what the vision is and how to interpret it to his/her own constituency. We educate those communicators of the brand in the power of retail thinking – in the power of re-education.
- REevolve: we believe in continuous evolution of the retail brand.
- REstorm: retail brainstorming.
- REvitalization: bringing new energy to the brand through retail thinking and application.
- REflagging: using the power of a flagship concept store to your retail efforts.
- REstoring: bringing your ethics alive within your retail efforts,

Appendix 2:
How to succeed by knowing what's going on

There are a few sources of constantly updated inspiration that we feel are invaluable daily tools. We highly recommend them:

- howtosucceedatretail.com – an accompanying website for readers of this book which will allow you to access many more regularly updated strategies, cases, tools and methodologies to help you succeed at retail even more.
- springwise.com
- brandchannel.com
- trendwatching.com

Appendix 3:
How to succeed by referencing

We invite you to access the many references we have used throughout this book – they are all invaluable.

10 best.com
Ad Age 2006, Data sourced from Ad Age (USA); additional content by WARC staff
adage.com (2006) Millions of US dollars advertising spend
AP (2006) Wal-Mart tries to improve fashion trends, Friday 10 November, by Anne D'Innocenzio, AP Business Writer, Wal-Mart's challenge is convincing shoppers to buy fashion instead of just the basics
Alex Wipperfürth (alex@plan-b.biz) is a partner at marketing boutique Plan B in San Francisco. The Red Bull case study is an excerpt from his book *Brand Hijack* (Portfolio, Pengiun Group, 2005)
Anderson, Chris (2006) *The Long Tail*, Hyperion
Arnold, S J (2002) Lessons learned from the world's best retailers, *International Journal of Retail & Distribution Management*, **30** (11), pp 562–70
Carney, Beth (2005) Dyson's magic carpet ride, *BusinessWeek*, April [Online], www.businessweek.com/bwdaily/dnflash/apr2005/nf2005041_
Chan Kim, W and Mauborgne, Renée (2005) *Blue Ocean Strategy*, HBS Press
criticaleye.com

Culturebox (2006) Is Whole Foods wholesome? The dark secrets of the organic-food movement. By Field Maloney, posted 17 March [Online], www.culture-box.com

Daily Telegraph (2006a), Business news, 27 February

Daily Telegraph (2006b) The Supermarket is born, 20 March

Dutta, Devangshu (2005) Retail @ the speed of fashion, imagesfashion [Online] www.imagesfashion.com/back/profile/july03_5_profile_retail_speed_fashion.htm (accessed 11 October 2005)

Economist (2005) Consumer power – power at last, *Economist*, 31 March [Online], www.economist.com/displaystory.cfm?story_id=3810230 (accessed 22 September 2005)

Economist (2006a) The behemoth from Bentonville, 25 February

Economist (2006b) Foreign retailers mount an onslaught on India, and local companies fight back, *The Economist* print edition, 2 November

Economist (2006c) King content, Don't write off Hollywood and the big media groups just yet, *The Economist* print edition, 19 January

FT (2006) Tesco uses its noodle to attract Chinese shoppers, *Financial Times*, 16 September

Gladwell, Malcolm (2002) *The tipping point*, Blackwell, London

Gladwell, Malcolm (2006) *Blink*, Penguin, Harmondsworth

Glengarry Glen Ross, a 1992 film, distributed by New Line Cinema, based on the 1984 Pulitzer Prize and Tony-winning play of the same name by David Mamet. Mamet also adapted the play into the screenplay for the film.

Grocer (2006) Branding: where now for own labels? 25 November

IHT (2006a), Britain leads the way in Internet advertising, *International Herald Tribune*, 3 December

IHT (2006b) Buyers want it to be all about 'me', by Shelley Emling, *International Herald Tribune*, Friday, 20 January

IHT (2006c) How to succeed in retailing – by really trying, by Barbara Wall, *International Herald Tribune*, 1 April

IHT (2006d) Moscow money, rich Russians are spending as if there's no tomorrow – which many say there won't be, by Masha Gessen, *International Herald Tribune*, 13 October

IHT (2006e) Placement blog to blog, *International Herald Tribune*, 4 December

IHT(2006f) Trade imbalance masks a struggle to get by in China, by Thomas Fuller, *International Herald Tribune*, 3 August

In-Store Metrics Consortium (2006), September 2006, published October 2006, In-Store Marketing Institute

Jon Edge (2006) Will the brand get diluted?, by Jon Edge, Senior Designer, Wolff Olins

Kathleen Squires NEW YORK SHOPPING [Online], http://nymag.com/listings/stores

Kapferrer, Jean Noel (2006) DLF Conference, Stockholm

Karmaloop.com – http://www.karmaloop.com

Klein, Naomi (2001) *No Logo*, Flamingo, London

Mandmeurope.com (2006) Data sourced from mandmeurope.com; additional content by WARC staff, 14 November 2006

Marketing Week (2006) Top Employer Survey, 23 November

McKinsey (2006) USA: The media traditional TV advertising is losing efficacy, McKinsey

Michalko, Michael (1992) *Thinkertoys*, Ten Speed Press

Motley Fool (2006) H&M: In style around the world, by Matt Koppenheffer, 10 November

Mr Web.com, Data sourced from MrWeb.com (UK); additional content by WARC staff

Natlallergy (2005) Dyson DC15 the ball – animal, national allergy [Online], www.natlallergy.com/allergy_relief/1662/dyson-dc15-the-ball-animal-hepa-vacuum.html (accessed 10 October 2005)

Price, Mark and Hastings, Steve (2004a) *Money can't buy loyalty*, Admap, 447, February

Price, Mark and Hastings, Steve (2004b) *Rethinking the Future*, Admap

PSFK: '4C: The View From Here' is a new regular section on PSFK where they ask senior execs in a myriad of industries what cultural trends are facing their business today

Rethinking Retail: The Superquinn Experience by Rowan Gibson [Online], www.rethinkinggroup.com/rowan/InspirationSuperquinn.htm

Springwise (2004) Retail focus: only for dads and tweens, Springwise Newsletter, 17, September/October [Online], www.springwise.com/newsletters/SEP04/newsletter.htm (accessed 22 September 2005)

Springwise (2005a) Brand spaces, Springwise.com [Online], www.springwise.com/newbusinessideas/redLounge.htm (accessed 22 September 2005)

Springwise (2005b) Coming to a village near you, Springwise.com [Online], www.springwise.com/newbusinessideas/2003/08/london_fashion_bus.html (accessed 22 September, 2005)

Springwise (2005c) Mobile merchandise, Springwise.com [Online], www.springwise.com/newbusinessideas/2003/08/london_fashion_bus.html (accessed 22 September, 2005)

Springwise (2005d) Perfume meets retail theater, Springwise Newsletter, 21, April [Online], www.springwise.com/newsletter/previous_21.html (accessed 26 September 2005)

Springwise (2005e) Really super fast pizza, Springwise.com, April [Online], www.springwise.com/newbusinessideas/superFastPizza.htm (accessed 27 September 2005)

Sunday Times (2006a) Science cracks the code of the crazy shopper, Jonathan Leake, Science Editor, 23 April

Sunday Times (2006b), The GREEN grocers, 24 September

Superquinn: The Superquinn Experience by Rowan Gibson, author of *Rethinking the Future* [Online], www.rethinkinggroup.com/rowan/ InspirationSuperquinn.htm

Times (2006a) Ask the expert: Maurice Saatchi on advertising, 19 June

Times (2006b) Cameras help Tesco, 4 October

Times (2006c) Tesco proves its world class credentials, 4 October

Trendwatching (2005a) Being spaces, trendwatching.com [Online], www.trendwatching.com/trends/2002/11/BEINGSPACES.html (accessed 22 September 2005)

Trendwatching (2005b) Pop-up retail, trendwatching.com [Online], www.trendwatching.com/trends/POPUP_RETAIL.htm (accessed 26 September 2005)

Trendwatching (2005c) Tryvertising, trendwatching.com [Online], www.trendwatching.com/trends/TRYVERTISING.htm (accessed 27 September 2005)

USA Today (2006) WFM, 28 June 2006

WSJ (2005) Shelf promotion: in a shift, marketers beef up ad spending inside stores; Funky displays and lighting, TV spots in Wal-Mart; Unsettling Madison Avenue; Fake doorknobs pitch diapers, by Emily Nelson and Sarah Ellison, *Wall Street Journal* (Eastern Edition), New York, 21 September, p A.1

Index